Fragmented Reality
Part 1: Domino Effect

The Negative

He appears out of nowhere
I flinch
His silhouette has the same shades of color
as the skyline of New York
Muddled.
Fuzzy.
Multicolored.
His face that night outside
Sends chills down my spine
But caresses my insides
Maybe he is just misunderstood
Or maybe he is a wolf under that hood
He appears out of nowhere inside my mind
The outline of shades of dark colors
Blurred.
Turned upside down
I flinch, I close my eyes, I cry
I wish I could relive those moments
In a reality that were actually benign

Cover Artwork by M. Waqas

Introduction

They say time heals all wounds. But time has not been my best friend in this story. In fact, it has been my worst enemy. Due to time and bad timing, I had to endure the worst episode of self-doubt, vulnerability, invalidation and complacency that I have ever experienced in my life.

Some people could claim that unrequited love is one of the most powerful sensations ever. But I would argue that it is the aspect of *unrequited* or *unreciprocated kindness* to that unrequited love that makes that sensation even more painful. Putting *that* aside, just imagine adding in a very dark and distorted perception of reality into the mixture. It indeed takes that kind of pain to another level.

October 15-16 2023. I will NEVER forget that weekend. I will never forget those dates. I traveled to New Jersey to unwind and have some fun with a dating app companion. The experience ultimately left a lot to be desired. I admit, I desperately hoped to hook up with someone else in order to make the best out of that weekend. I don't have enough of that in my life. I grew up extremely religious, reserved and timid. I am now at 32 years old barely trying to navigate life and the world of dating. I am just now learning how to cope with this world itself.

Coincidentally that same weekend, I ended up meeting someone else who was my Facebook friend (and follower?) for about seven to eight years. For some context, on social media I have dedicated a good portion of my life (a little over a decade) advocating for linguistic and cultural rights pertaining to his region of origin—North Africa. So naturally, I assumed that there was already a level of respect and appreciation that he had towards me. Even if it was just minimal. All these years I did somewhat have a crush on him but on an extremely basic subconscious level. The odd thing is I could recall so many specific things about him, his posts and his personality. I am usually very good at reading people. I am good with patterns. I can usually tell a lot about someone just by how they come across online. And honestly, my intuition over the years did tell me to stay away from him. His overbearingly and obnoxiously pompous attitude would radiate from his Facebook profile. Despite feeling this way towards him and knowing this information, something about him still intrigued me enough to one day meet him. I would actually even keep tabs (again on a strictly subconscious level) whenever he would react or comment on my posts. Which was rare, but you see that's the point. If he hardly ever interacted with me, why do I recall paying attention to his attention to me? I can recall fixating on his display picture the moment he would view one of my Stories on Facebook. Almost as if those memories were meant to foreshadow what was to come in the future... So strange.

He once commented on a Story: "Beautiful eyes." I was delighted. Flattered.

He said exactly that to me that night too. It was a sweet moment actually that I replay in my head till this day. I was still sitting on the hotel bed waiting for him to make a move. And just when I thought nothing was going to happen, he comes over to me and gives me a hug and then he says, "Okay its getting late..see you!"—then steals a kiss from me. Yes, perhaps extremely cheesy and cliché for many, but for me it was the first time experiencing something that felt so seductively genuine. I then immediately kissed him back passionately. Firmly. Without any hesitation. It was my *first* time doing that with so much confidence with someone. He was someone I felt that I really knew. So it felt so natural to do that with him. No one has ever told me that I had beautiful eyes in the manner in which he did. Not in person. Not like that. I was actually pleasantly surprised when I met him in person. From the moment I met him till the moment he left, he was charming, attentive and considerate. He still had that kind of pretentious persona, but I wasn't that bothered by it. I just felt that was his way of being confident. I told myself: "Wow, I misjudged this person all this time!"

Remember that last line please.

That night was probably just a friendly fling for him. I get it. It was for me too. By that I mean a friendly encounter between two people. Or perhaps we were just strangers? I could not figure that out.

He did however reassure me that I did indeed know him better and more than the guy from the dating app I went to visit. "We have known each other for about seven years on Facebook, of course you know me more than him!" he said.

I was shy, nervous, anxious, insecure and most importantly humble. I was humble towards him. I didn't automatically assume he wanted some physical interaction. I hoped for it sure, but I wasn't sure he would find me attractive. I am glad he did. I was so happy to be in his presence. I have had nothing but horrible experiences with men. He was my best experience so far. He even told me he was shy himself. I didn't expect him to be a little socially awkward. I thought that was extremely adorable.

Keep this last line in mind please.

Though I had the chance to completely change my fate that day, I did not do so. I should have taken a 4:24 p.m. flight back to my home state, but I did not want to deal with staying overnight at an airport or getting a voucher for a nearby hotel. I know that was supposed to be something incredibly simple to do, but I struggle with severe anxiety and symptoms of overthinking, panic attacks and things of that sort. I was anxious about doing something unfamiliar.

Oh the irony…

I ended up being incredibly anxious about *doing* someone unfamiliar. We never actually had that many interactions prior. Especially not in a flirtatious nature. Remember, he was technically in between being a stranger and someone I knew. I couldn't easily make up my mind; everything happened so fast. (Well…*that* part was actually not so fast, it was nice and steady haha.)

But for that reason precisely, I was really awkward too. I even had a little April Kepner moment with him. Remember that episode on Grey's Anatomy where April and Alex Karev were in their dorm about to have sex and April says, "Wait, please could we go a little slower?" And Alex replied rudely: "What do want from me? Do you want to screw? Let's screw! If not get out! I'm not going to *hold your virgin hand and walk you through* it!" Only he and I would know why that particular scene would hilariously describe our little moment there. It's not that I was a virgin of course, and I sure as hell did not ask him to stop or go slower. (Haha, fuck no!) It was the fact that I clearly demonstrated a lack of experience. And although I had the courage to lean in and kiss him with all my might with no problem, I was still extremely shy and not so confident in doing other things in bed with him. But that did not seem to

5

bother him I think. And so I did appreciate his *patience, kindness* and *respect* there unlike the *ruthless* Alex Karev from the show.

Keep all of that in mind as this story unfolds…

1.The Catalyst

So what propelled me to write this book? Why write a book with an unconventional structure? Is this an essay? A non-fiction dark romance story? Or is this a book of poetry? It may be a distorted mixture of all of the above. The section where I do provide my "poetic" literary works are reserved at the end of this book. These are the events that gave birth to it all:

When I came back home from my trip, things felt like usual I guess. Only for some reason I felt like he was more serious than before. Then about a day or two, I saw something that made my stomach turn in all sorts of directions!

"In a relationship with Nahara Ruskin."

I was of course severely confused. I did what any woman would do in my position: Check out her profile. She seemed like a sweet woman. Immediately looking at her photo it brought joy to my heart. I began to gather as many details as possible as I could about her. She is a belly dancer and yoga instructor, an animal lover and she loves nature. She is very much into holistic health, and energy healing. Among the other info that I could gather, it seemed to me that she was an empath like me. (I sometimes avoid using this term since I feel it is overused, but my point is she and I seemed like two very sensitive people.) I could not process what I was seeing in front of me very well. I could not process it at all actually.

Despite me seeing a photo of them together exactly that same weekend (literally a day before we hooked up), it didn't automatically concern me too much since they did not seem that romantic with each other. It was a public gathering with other friends and family after all. I do not know how I began to rationalize this, but I somehow came to the conclusion that they were just friends, or at least in some sort of open relationship? At first I honestly thought she was some sort of celebrity or well known personality in her area that I thought the relationship status was just a joke. She seemed very professional and I thought it was odd to see her in a relationship with someone so…volatile. I simply did not know how to process that information. What I do know is that I started to feel a void inside of me every time I would speak to someone else on a dating app. My mind would come back to him. It was really important for me to not get carried away with assumptions. So the thought of those two being together ended there.

I then started to pay more attention to his profile, posts and comments than before. He honestly didn't seem to mind.

A good amount of time went by and it was around mid-November when I started to feel this incessant urge to talk to him again. To be more specific, I needed to see him again.

But all of a sudden my insecurities got the best of me, and I began to doubt if he enjoyed being with me or not.

To test this hypothesis, I decided to try to flirt with him a little to see if he was indeed interested in seeing me again.

The first attempt I admit, was incredibly cringe.

Out of nowhere I told him, "Man I need more sex in my life."

To which he replied: "Yeah we all do."

I hated myself in that moment. Who says something so weird like that? And yes, honestly I was annoyed at his dry delivery of a response, but that's the way he has always carried himself. I don't think he was that bothered by my message?

I shrugged it off and days later I noticed he "loved" reacted to a video of my cat. I know this will sound silly, but I felt butterflies in my stomach like a kid in high school. I felt some relief that I didn't scare him away with my previous comment.

That prompted me to be a little more comfortable with messaging him knowing that I was not bothering him.

The second attempt was me asking him if he thought I was attractive that night? He responded. "Yes you were."

My heart was at rest. I was more than satisfied. It felt so good to have his attention. It felt amazing.

Even more amazing when I caught him looking at my Facebook stories a day or two after my last question. My eyes were smiling seductively. I took those pictures for him.

More time went by and the more I felt disillusioned and underwhelmed with the men I would talk to on dating apps, the more I began to feel more and more attached to him. Not in *that* way just yet. I just really wanted to kiss him and do all sorts of nice things to him. The things that I was too shy to do that night. It was a mixture of lust (Do people still use that word?) excitement, curiosity and admiration with a hint of innocent passion. But due to my insecurity, I just felt that wasn't necessarily mutual. I knew I was the only one experiencing these emotions intensely.

But unfortunately, there was this odd "push and pull" force going on inside of me. I tried posting more photos and posts to get his attention but to no avail. At the same time, I couldn't help feel jealous at the other women he would respond to sometimes even with "heart" reacts, while with me he would respond with just "likes." I know that may sound stupid. But why *discriminate* among your friends? The actions we do, no matter how minimal send a message. Especially with written communication I am very analytical. So to me it felt almost intentional. I had a tooth extraction done and it was brutal. I posted pictures of myself in pain and with bruises all over my face. I expected a "shock" react from him at least. But instead he "shock" reacted to a post about a snow storm from another woman who happens to share the same Facebook nickname as I only spelled differently—Thasrith Nunzar. This translates to the "Bride of the Rain" in his native language Tamazight. I know that may sound strange, but we both use it as a nickname based on North African folklore or ancient mythology. So her post was about a snow storm. So what? She was just fine. She didn't go to work that day. Big deal! I on the other hand was in a lot of pain from nerve damage. I don't mean to sound *childish.* But I just couldn't resist this sensation I was feeling. It was not just the fact that I was feeling jealous, but I was also questioning if maybe I was *annoying* him in any way? Maybe he *regretted* meeting me that night? That concerned me.

My concerns only got worse after my third attempt at flirting with him. He posted a picture of a bottle that to me looked like white wine. So I messaged him saying: "Haha, would be so nice to have a glass of white wine with you one night." To which he responded: It's not white wine, its olive oil." No emojis. No "haha." He sounded really serious and annoyed. I felt mortified. So mortified. Obviously we all know what I was trying to imply with that *double entendre.* I immediately deleted all those messages, and I apologized and said: "How embarrassing! Sorry! I *guess I was seeing things that were*

9

not there!! I always find myself in these situations!" He was supposed to pick up on that particular subtext, but I do not think he did. He replied back by saying it wasn't a big deal and that mistakes happen. I still could not get over the awkwardness of it all. So much I even remember posting on my wall: "Ouch…Damn! That hurt more than my tooth extraction!" I'm not so sure if he ever noticed that. I did notice however, Nahara also liked and commented on that same post. But mysteriously I was not able to see that post anymore on his account after the fact. Either he deleted it, or he made it not visible for me by adjusting his audience setting. Bizarre. I then decided from that point on to stop interacting with him and to try to get him off my mind completely.

But then suddenly… some time in mid-December, I posted a picture of a post workout. I was laying on the bed showing a lot of cleavage in my sports bra. He liked that picture. I mean, you know he reacted with a like. It's incredible how something so simple as getting his attention again lifted me up. I took that as a sign that he was still thinking about me. That confidence boost definitely helped me gain the courage to finally ask him directly if he would ever be interested in meeting me again. Four days later on December 26, 2023, I messaged him: "Hey Merry Christmas. You know I really *miss you,* and I was wondering if I were to visit you, would you like to see me again? He immediately replied back saying, "Yeah just let me know when you're around." I was ecstatic. I haven't been that happy in a long time. It felt like being under him and under his breath was just right around the corner. And again, at this point I didn't feel anything else other what I described earlier. Mind you, I used "I miss you." I was concerned to how he would react to that. But honestly at that moment I just meant I missed his company, and I assumed that's exactly how he interpreted it too. Since he did not react negatively to that and he did NOT hesitate to accept my request, I assumed everything was going to be just fine.

Time went by and all I could think of was seeing him again. It became the only thing I was looking forward to. I started to work out more and pay more attention to my skincare routine. I planned how I was going to wear my makeup the next time I were to see him, and I was already shopping for different cute outfits that he would find me beautiful in.

But yet again that "push and pull" factor began to resurface.

As much as I tried to stop myself from getting that attached to him. It was too late. We all know what serotonin, dopamine and oxytocin does to the infatuated mind.

Hours had become days and the days became weeks and the weeks led to the month of January when I finally had to admit it to myself: I fell madly in love with this person. I believe I did fall madly in love with him the moment I saw him. *Coup de foudre* as they call it in French. Why you may ask?

I'm not sure, maybe when my eyes locked eyes with his and his smile that first night we were together, it felt as if nothing else mattered. In his eyes I saw innocence. I saw that little kid inside who was misunderstood. I know what I saw. It felt as if I have known him for centuries. As if the past and present and future were combined in that moment. I felt like I knew him from a past lifetime. I felt like I could get to know him even better in the present, and I felt like I could spend my entire future with him. But I had suppressed these thoughts in order to protect myself from precisely getting hurt.

Oh the unfortunate irony…

Yet again, on a particular post all of his comments comprised of females and only my comment was liked and the rest were hearted. It felt like he really wanted me out of the picture. Literally.

But was there a simpler and more logical explanation behind all of that? I mean, what have I done to make him uncomfortable? It was mid-January and I attended a cultural event in Boston. Since it is one that occurs every year pertaining to his ethnic background, I precisely attended so that I would see him again. I figured that was the perfect opportunity for us to have some innocent fun again. I asked him why he couldn't attend. I specifically said "I was waiting for you to *join me* here at the event." He replied by saying "That was the plan! But work got in the way and I'm planning a trip to Morocco. I will stop by Germany and England along the way." "I have not missed that event in 11 years, this would be my first time!" He sounded friendly this time. He was really happy about the trip. I shrugged it off and just hoped for us to eventually meet one day! And once again, I caught him one last time before he took his trip taking a peek at my Facebook story of myself smiling seductively. And of course, I took that picture for him. But the more I still tried to interact with his posts and pictures, the more I felt he would purposely try to make me feel ignored. He would "like" my comments while he "heart" reacted to other comments that had basically the same content in regards to the New Year and his trip. I also vividly remember I "liked" a post in Arabic regarding politics in the Middle East. I can speak and especially read and understand Classical Arabic fluently. He made that post hidden or deleted it after I had liked it. I didn't understand why. So at that point, I was getting very confused. I could feel it in my gut he was treating me differently on purpose. And in the deepest part of my mind, I was already coming up with so many possibilities. But I did not allow them to surface (just yet). Until…

"Have fun honey!" She commented on one of his posts.

My heart not only sank, it almost imploded like a submarine worth billions of dollars. This woman, who was this woman? He had most of his likes and comments from females more than men. He had total womanizer or player vibes written all over him all these years. I would see him post about his trips, his night outs to clubs and bars and girls in bikinis all the time. His status, her comment, the mere idea of him being in a serious relationship just did not make sense! All these years I had this specific idea of who he was. Despite his reputation, I did not think of him lowly. Just a man being a man! But I sure did not want my mind to wonder in another direction about him, about her and about that night. I was growing impatient however. I needed to tell him how I felt. I had of course my reservations. I feared that if he knew how I felt, he would then not want to see me again. I recorded myself over 30 times more or less. (I opted for a prerecorded voice message over one that is done on the spot on Messenger.) I tried to get the right words. I was meticulous. I was careful.

I was frightened, but I was calm. I was confused about so many things about him, but I was *grounded* in my feelings. I knew exactly what I felt and why. I thought about his time and schedule. I precisely waited until he came back from his trip so that I knew I wouldn't be bothering him.

On January 28, 2024, (yet another date I will not forget) I sent him a seven-minute voice message. Skipping the intro, the main part of my message went something like this:

"…I feel almost as if I…as if I love you. But I don't expect anything in return. I just needed you to know that you are unique. I wish I could be in your arms again, If I could just have two seconds in them, I'd be the happiest woman alive.

I just wanted you to know, you are amazing and you have all the qualities Im looking for. Whoever you choose to be with I hope you are happy and you deserve all the happiness and success in your life. I pray that I will find someone like you. If I had someone like you, I would never let him go, I would never take him for granted. I want you to know that I don't take you nor our friendship for granted."

(Note: By "whoever you choose to be with," I was honestly speaking in general. No one in specific. I believe I was trying very hard not to think about Nahara, but she was inevitably on the back of my mind. I also said "someone *like you*," and not "him" literally. I wanted to make it clear I wasn't after him for a relationship or anything of that sort. I was just trying to make him feel flattered and good about himself.)

That sounded pretty profound wouldn't you think so? I meant every word. I remember exactly my state of mind in that moment.

Out of fear and insecurity, I delivered that message with the assumption that he absolutely did not feel the same for me. My intention was just to make him feel flattered that someone beautiful, intelligent and pure hearted like me was capable of feeling this for him. And I must emphasize: I sent this message under the assumption that he was single in my version of reality. What followed thereafter, also happened still me assuming he was a single man. Please keep this in mind.

He blocked me the next day. Without saying a word.

Oh the cruel irony…

I precisely told him at the end of my message "Please do not block me." I said that out of humility. I said a lot of things out of humility or *insecurity* rather. I also said: "I do not take you nor our friendship for granted." And yet, that action alone of blocking someone without giving them an explanation would be considered taking someone not only for granted, but also diminishing that person's worth into smithereens. Wouldn't you agree? This small gesture. It told me everything!

It was extremely shocking for me in that moment. Out of all the reactions I imagined from him, that was the last one on my list. I never thought he would actually do that *without apologizing first and saying goodbye.*

I precisely tried to phrase my words so that I wouldn't sound too crazy. I thought if I sounded like I was dying to marry him and have his kids then that would have definitely scared him away. But all I wanted was to share a philosophical epiphany with him, about him. Was that not how I came across?

I did not deserve to be dismissed or ignored in that manner.

I had to get to the bottom of this, so I used another Facebook account in order to send him all sorts of messages.

I also got his attention by posting on his public profile: "Hey look at your other inbox folder/hidden inbox." (Because he was not getting notified otherwise). Yeah, that was definitely taking a risk. But I had no other option unfortunately.

My first couple of sentences were polite but demanding an explanation in a frantic manner. I was deeply saddened, yet extremely livid over how he reacted.

Furthermore, I took a screenshot of him "haha" reacting to a stupid meme after he blocked me. On a mutual friend's profile I was able to see the missing person behind the reaction and I knew immediately it was him. It stings to think about it because the implication is: he heard my voice message, thought it was incredibly stupid or irrational and decided the best way to deal with that was to never see me or hear from me again. Meaning that decision did not hurt him or faze him one bit, but rather caused him *relief* and *excitement.* Think about it. Who gets blocked with the expectation of *eventually getting unblocked?* In that kind of a context? No one with common sense. Perhaps that does occur, and it is not out of the realm of possibilities, but especially between men and women that rarely happens.

Ergo, it absolutely made perfect sense to message him with that screenshot in that moment along with my other choice of words afterwards. He did NOT react well to my messages at all! He replied:

"I DON'T HAVE TIME FOR THIS CHILDISH SHIT."

Ouch. Yup. Ouch... is actually an understatement on how I actually felt.

Well, blocking me without saying a word to me beforehand proved that I meant absolutely nothing to him in that moment. There was simply no other way I could have reacted and there was no other conclusion I could have come up with during that conversation. That small little gesture alone made me realize I was a joke to him this whole time. Perhaps I was a joke to him all these years? I knew for a fact he was NEVER going to unblock me which meant we were NEVER going to see each other again. Of course I was going to be extremely upset! I was extremely blinded at the reality of the situation that his gaslighting effects were starting to kick in. I began to regret sending him those messages. I thought maybe I was in the wrong and I could have changed up my tone? I could have said something differently?

I remember thinking: I did NOT begin my messages with profanities. I actually stated how can someone who I thought was kind deep down inside could be that cruel to block someone without at least an explanation?

Ergo, demonstrating my level of maturity there. Had I been ANY other woman truly embodying childish behavior I would have attacked him using all sorts of insults. And although I got upset and gave him an attitude like anyone humiliated and shocked would, I did not use any ad hominem attacks towards his character.

For that alone, I deserved more respect and kindness from him. Doesn't that make sense?

"I just wanna be left alone, I have problems to deal with. I don't have time for this!"

"Let me respect you, when you do that I will unblock you."

Yes. This sounds somewhat respectful. But let's not forget the entire context here. Where was *my* respect when he decided to not take my feelings for him seriously? Where was *my* respect when he blocked me as if I weren't someone real and someone he once touched? Where was *my* respect when he didn't offer me the apology that I deserved? Where was *my* respect from the very beginning of this journey?

"Stop chasing me around!" he said.

"Stop talking about your feelings, I'm honestly not interested."

"Please go find somebody else in your town!"

When asked if he lied about wanting to meet me a second time he replied: "Yeah, I changed my mind like humans do!"

Me: "Because of my recording?"

Him: "No I just want to be left alone fuuuck. I don't have time for this shit please. Go away!"

Damn…Fuck.. What the hell? Shit.. What the actual….F…

I was bawling at this point. Crying hysterically.

He did not give a shit about my pain.

Why would a man like that be worth my tears at this point you may ask?

I was either unreasonably stubborn as fuck or a sad masochist.

Or both?

Sure…all of the above I guess. But in reality I was still very much in love with him, and I kept trying to rationalize everything. On one hand, I should have seen this coming I told myself. I should have never sent him that voice message. Or perhaps he was planning on blocking me either way? Maybe he was just pretending to be kind and patient with me because he felt sorry for me? Which is in itself very bizarre because he wouldn't be the type to sugar coat things. I mean obviously not, hence his particular choice of words above. Either way ladies and gentleman, what this man did to me right in that moment was incredibly fucked up.

"Thank you for your feelings, but I'm not interested, leave me alone and mature up a bit." He said. Was that supposed to be the part where he thought he was being *kind*?

Oh Fuck that! First of all, I already knew he wasn't interested. That was the the whole fucking point of my existentialist metaphysical hasheesh-infused philosophical monologue in my voice message that day. He DID NOT have to rub it my fucking face in that manner. Second of all, I didn't need his mediocre gratitude alongside his ad hominem comments. I needed *humility* back. I needed an apology. But I guess that was too much to ask?

The self-entitlement. The arrogance. The sheer audacity of this man! Why?

Why would he expect me to be that passive and accept his condescension and rudeness as if I deserved it?

I could not understand, but at that time I was incredibly stubborn and I NEEDED to attempt to get inside his mind to try to understand his choices.

I thought maybe he was offended by how I approached him. Maybe he was just under a lot of stress that day he unintentionally took out his anger out on me?

Contemplation.

Never underestimate the power of contemplation. Reflection. Analyzing. Reviewing and Revising.

Exhibit A—"Yeah I changed my mind like humans do."

Yes oh wise protagonist of my story, you are absolutely right.

Humans do and can change their minds at any time.

Usually however, when certain plans change, out of COURTESY it is customary to say "I am sorry."

"I am (very) sorry" were the only four words I was looking for that day we last contacted each other. Not "I love you (too)."

Fuck! How could he not understand that I was extremely hurt? I could not comprehend at that time.

I am a beautiful woman (I suppose?). At least to him I thought I was that night? So this beautiful woman was *really* looking forward to meeting him again so they could exchange fluids, and not mean words to one another. I thought he was looking forward for that too? I was not some child throwing a tantrum. I was a woman missing her *friend*. A woman willing to forget or suppress her feelings for good just to be able to be with him again at least for one more night. I never wanted a serious relationship with this crazy fool. I knew better than that based on my prior experiences with men like him. I just wanted something casual. I thought he really wanted to fuck me again too. That was the part that stung the most—the realization that he was NOT looking forward in meeting me at all. This idea then prompted other ideas to follow in this agonizing ripple effect that was taking place inside of me. Why then not block me before? Why then decide to sleep with me in the first place? Why wasn't I important enough for him to at least end our friendship on GOOD TERMS. Fuck...!!!

I fell in love with him for who he is, and not for what he can offer me or what he possesses. I fell in love with someone I thought who was kind. I remember his gaze. I remember his awkwardness. How can someone like that have ill intentions? How can someone with kind eyes be this despotic and two-faced I thought?

Indeed never underestimate the power of contemplation...

Subsequently after that, it was one Facebook account after another. For the record, I did not start creating new accounts. They were created ages ago. Apart from my main account where we were friends for years and the one where we last spoke to each other, the third one I began to use out of pure curiosity. I swear. I had NO intentions of messaging him. Four months went by after we last spoke with each other and when had our argument. FOUR! That's a long time isn't it? I actually thought that he could have possibly forgotten about the whole thing. My intention was to possibly start all over? Conduct a "reset" on my brain if you will? I thought if we just started to interact like old Facebook friends like before I would get over these feelings somehow? I don't know. I just knew I had no intention of flooding his inbox every again!

But..unfortunately...that did not happen. And that my friends is the understatement of the century........

I had commented on some of Thasrith's posts, and I posted a comment on another mutual friend's profile. Yes, I was obviously trying to get him to notice me, but again I DID NOT message him or talk to him first. As soon as he saw my profile, he panicked and blocked me. I actually have no idea what could have been his thought process. He either panicked, or as soon as he saw my picture he recoiled in disgust? Was I that despicable to him that he couldn't stand the sight of me?

Why so much anger?

Why so much aggression towards me?

Was he *guilty* of something?

Did he just wanted to avoid me messaging him and having another frantic conversation?

I'll be honest. What triggered me the most was noticing him reacting to Thasrith's posts with "heart" reacts again while I remained blocked. Something came over me. An unbearable sensation of jealousy, rage, confusion and desperation altogether.

I needed to get him to talk to me no matter what because the nature of this situation did not make any sense to me. Why treat her with more respect? Why was I treated like I was not only beneath him but *beneath a woman like her*? But at that point I was not aware of the reality just yet, I just needed to know why he decided to block me in an instant as if he never knew me! As if he really hated me…

So on this account my messages actually began with an apology if I used the wrong tone or if I said the wrong things to upset him that day of our argument.

I begged him for closure. I even used the word "implored" for fuck sakes. That was me waiving a white flag of surrender. But I also needed to stand my ground and try to desperately convince him where he was wrong. At the end I remember

21

saying things along the lines of: " I am not well, I need closure. I need to end things in *good terms.* I just wanted for us to say goodbye in a positive manner. I can't handle the cognitive dissonance of you being kind at first to then having that last argument. Please I kindly and humbly request you apologize to me too for the way you acted and I promise I will leave you alone for good."

Unfortunately all of my efforts were futile.

He blocked me yet again.

From that moment I gave up and the only thing that kept me going was finishing this book.

Here is the problem: *cognitive dissonance.*

Yes. I could not not handle the cognitive dissonance between the man I fell in love with that night with the man who was treating me like utter trash. Remember the specific lines from my intro? Compare and contrast that to this incident. I tried so hard to see things from his perspective. I really did try. But that whole situation was just really bizarre, shocking and unfair for me. It took only a seven-minute voice message to completely change his behavior towards me. While I completely understand the effect it had on him, I did not understand the unreciprocated or unrequited kindness from him. I thought to myself: "*Why react so aggressively to profound thoughts*?" Why react so hatefully to a kind soul like me? Why was I not deserving of a proper and gentle "goodbye?" On one hand I felt esteemed by him all these years, and I felt desired by him that one night. Was I just not good enough? Was I too beneath him? Did I annoy him THAT much? My goodness that "THIS IS CHILDISH I DON'T HAVE TIME FOR THIS SHIT STOP CHASING ME AROUND-GO AWAY LEAVE ME ALONE" just hits very differently now when

I think about his demeanor just a week prior to our argument. As I mentioned above, we spoke to each other just fine like genuine friends a week before this happened! He completely changed in such an extremely short amount of time. The irony was I thought I had good timing. Like I said, time has not been my friend. Fuck time and fuck my life!

And who the fuck was he to use me like his punching bag and doormat that day? What was his excuse to block me yet again when I wasn't even "messaging him about my feelings?" I was just using another account minding my own God damn business commenting on my friend's profile who was someone I knew for 11 years. Much longer than I knew him. What was the problem?

How did I become all of a sudden so meaningless and unbearable to him in such a small amount of time?

We were *friends* right?

What was it that he emphasized to me that night?

"We have been friends for *seven* years. Of course you KNOW me MORE than that other guy."

Is that right?

How many times did we talk prior to that night?

A proper and meaningful conversation on messenger? Only once.

How many times did I FaceTime the guy on the dating app prior to meeting him? 60 + times over the span of 1 year. We talked and talked and talked and we learned things about each other—things that him and I did not learn over 7-8 years.

Of course my intuition knew that.

But I ignored it because I was desperately trying to have a good time with this person I believe. I think it was convenient for me as well to believe in the words that he was telling me.

But even then, it kills me in the inside to consider the possibility that the only reason he needed to say that to me was so that I can feel comfortable enough to sleep with him.

I wanted to understand what was the meaning behind our *friendship* all these years if showering him with compliments and good thoughts was all it took for him to take me for granted and unleash so much animosity towards me.

"Stop chasing me around" he said.

Jesus...Are you fucking kidding me?!

Sometime in the spring of 2019 I took a trip to New York and he noticed that on Facebook. He told me that if I were to ever be around his area in the east coast to let him know because he was interested in meeting me. I will never forget those words. I knew for a fact there was something deeper about me that he wanted to discover, not just the depth in between my thighs. I knew for a fact he has other ways to meet women and sleep with them. Therefore, I had to be more valuable to him than just for a one night stand. Right? Or...I mean...if he indeed struggles that much to get a good looking plus somewhat famous, (in his Moroccan community at least) plus intellectual woman to sleep with him, then why not show a little bit of gratitude for me at the end? Geez! How does someone just throw away a seven or potentially eight-year friendship like that? In fact sometime in 2018 or the year after, I vividly remember a time I posted something about animal abuse or animal cruelty awareness. It was a picture of a dog that got beaten up and he immediately messaged me saying: "Hey please, take down that post about the dog. I hate seeing that stuff on my feed. And I *would hate to block a friend like you."* I immediately said okay. I listened to him in a fucking heartbeat. I didn't protest. ANY other woman would have been offended and say: "No, I will not take it down because it is my profile and I can post whatever I want!" Nope. I did not say something like that. I was *respectful.*

And look where that got me.

He gave me an ultimatum then, why not give me an ultimatum that day? He could have told me to please stop messaging him about my feelings in a polite way and I would have stopped if that meant saving our friendship. I swear to God. But little did I know at that time, there was never a friendship to save to even begin with…

Parallel Universe #1

So I am about to present to you some "parallel universe" exercises. When I came up with this, I was still very much in shock and very much confused and very much not fully aware of the reality behind who he really was. Keep that in mind please. So this is how I would have imagined our conversation to unfold. This is what I desperately wanted him to say to me:

Me: Sends the voice message

Him: "Haha, that's cute…but I'm sorry I'm not interested in hearing about your feelings. It was very kind of you, but I have a lot of shit going on I don't have time for this stuff please."

That above ladies and gentlemen would have been A PERFECT way to respond to my message. Perfect. Why? Well, it's also condescending as fuck. BUT—It's a *playful* condescension. Harmless. It would have still stayed true to his speech pattern without compromising his cold, dry assertiveness. I swear to God I would have not had a problem with this.

Also, if I would have asked: "So, I'm assuming that also means you are no longer interested?"

He could have responded by:

Him: "Yeah, *sorry* I changed my mind, it would not be a good idea."

Me: "Is it because you found me that unattractive?"

Him: "Noo, you are great, wonderful but its just not a good idea sorry… please find someone else around ya I'm sure you will be fine. (In the original conversation, he did say I was "wonderful, great," although it sounded incredibly sarcastic or unauthentic given the intensity of the argument.)

Me: Ok. My voice message wasn't supposed to be taken THAT literally by the way. It's something my ex and I came up with when there was no more romantic love between us. We call it, 'love in humanity.' A love that is just supposed to be what a normal human being feels towards another human being. You love them no matter what and you just want them to be happy. I didn't mean to offend you."

Him: "I didn't say ya did anything I just need to be left alone pls and listen *I would hate to block someone like you* so stop with these msgs about your feelings."

Me: "Can I still be friends with you on Facebook and comment on your posts?"

Him: "of course ya can…"

No need for blocking, so no hard feelings. Not ad hominem attacks. No push back. His acknowledgment of my thoughts and feelings would have been the *mature* thing to do on his part and I would have accepted his request with no problem.

I would have preferred this version A MILLION times over our original heated conversation.

But would it still hurt me? Yes of course it would. I definitely would have felt it sting so badly in my insides, BUT at least the pain would have been like stepping on dry ice and not like having nitric acid shoved down your throat like how things actually unfolded between us.

Parallel Universe #2

So let's say after blocking me I end up sending him my original frantic message through that other account in the exact same fashion:

Me: "I thought our friendship meant something of value to you enough to tell me "its ok one day you will find the right person." I was not going to pester you with 'oh I want to marry you bla bla bla,' [Insert laughing emojis here.] I would have been ok dude lmao.' I'm just like any other girl your slept with and then developed feelings- boom! Blocked! Easy fix? Nah..lol I haven't felt so humiliated in a while. Never thought I'd be disposable to you." (Insert screenshot of him "haha" reacting to a meme after he blocked me.) "You think this is funny? How can you be laughing while I'm in pain??"

This is close to what I actually sent him. I am of course paraphrasing everything. My messages were really really long and I know the male brain is incapable of processing that (and I mean, understandably so). So for the sake of providing an example of what I actually wrote that day, I am giving you the phrases I believed triggered him to speak the way he did to me.

My thought process was: On one hand, it is clear as night and day I am extremely upset and I don't necessarily mean to sound like I am laughing about the situation. I did not mean to come across as if I were a lot younger than my own age. There is a context about myself that I did not share with him, and it would have hopefully justified my own particular speech pattern that I used that day. However, it is not uncommon for women even my age to be eccentrically sassy during arguments. Right? It's our defense mechanism so that we don't feel so hurt. It really is not supposed to be that deep. But see, since I am very inquisitive and analytical, I had a feeling I wouldn't be able to illicit the right response from him due to my choice of words and tone. That is where I believe things went wrong.

However, him being almost *a decade older than me*, should have had the choice *and the fucking maturity* to respond accordingly given the *entire context* of the situation.

He could have responded as such:

"You are blowing everything out of portion. Please stop.

<u>*I did not mean to hurt you.*</u> I just can't handle this shit right now. *I'm sorry* but I needed to block you. I will unblock you at the right time but I need ya to stop talking about your feelings I'm honestly not interested."

Me: "I was just trying to flatter you, not make you upset. I said that you were amazing… I wasn't trying to force you into a serious relationship. I was just trying to express a concept me and my ex came up with that has nothing to do with romantic love. It's called 'loving in humanity.' I said 'I loved you' in a humanitarian sense. It wasn't supposed to be taken that literally. I just wished the best things in your life because you were kind to me that night and I was just trying to be appreciative. That's all."

Him: "ok ok… I get it. Thank you, you too. I need to be left alone now please. And you are fucking wrong about what you're saying about me please have more common sense. I will unblock ya when you stop messaging me about your feelings."

Me: "Okay, so I guess that means we will never see each other gain?"

Him: " Yeah I changed my mind about that. *I'm sorry."* *Goodbye. OR:* "I just need ya to leave me alone for a while and then I will unblock you. *I am sorry."*

—2nd account blocked—

See, I could totally see a scenario where he could have controlled his anger just a bit since it should have been obvious to him that I was extremely hurt, and that is why I reacted the way I did. So he could have overlooked my particular speech pattern that could have come across as "childish" to someone of his age and be wiser and logical and just say what I proposed above. I should have not have been so harshly judged. He would have shown me his version of kindness by showing a little bit of *remorse.* But still being assertive, still a little cold so it would have not been out of the realm of possibilities due to his personality type.

I need to emphasize and state that I was merely assuming the MAIN reason why he thought I was being childish was because I was *doubting his good character.* In other words, he got extremely upset because instead of me understanding the real reason behind his choices, I decided to take it the wrong way. But that was mere speculation. At the time that I came up with this version of reality, this one in particular was my absolute favorite and the most plausible. I would have given ANYTHING to experience this alternate universe instead.

Parallel Universe #3

I sometimes wonder what would have happened if I had never sent that voice message but instead asked him this:

"Hey, so I am planning a trip to New Jersey again this October. That is actually purely coincidental. A friend a mine from New York is inviting me over, but I want to see you too. Are you still down?"

Him. "I'm not sure maybe.. message me then and I'll let ya know." OR "Yeah for sure. I will be waiting. Just message me when you are here."

I actually do not know. I have exhausted all possibilities in my brain I guess. I was just trying to figure out if the reason behind him changing his mind over meeting me had to do with me stating my feelings for him OR…

Ugh…

Ladies and gentlemen… There was and there is no parallel universe. While I know I am in the right, and I have a point in attempting to consider different possible outcomes that could have occurred on that day, the attempt itself was incredibly pointless and naive. Please do not feel insulted. That was not meant to be a waste of your valuable time. What I was trying to demonstrate was my ultimate deepest desire to turn back time. I wanted to invite you inside the first door to the agonizing labyrinth inside my brain that was attempting to cope with a series of intolerable realizations. I was repeating these outcomes in my head over and over for months. Speculating and imagining for months out of the purity and naiveness of my heart. I desperately needed to demonstrate to him that I was right, so I meticulously came up with powerful arguments to persuade him to apologize to me.

In vain. Futile. Sadly all meaningless in the end.

"I did not plan to develop these feelings. It hurts so much because I know there's nothing that I can do… I know it's a *dead* end. It can't lead to anything… I didn't expect to have these feelings. I'm sorry! I don't want these feelings I don't want to be in pain… The problem is, no other man will be enough. I will be looking for very specific qualities and the problem is…*you raised the bar of standards* really high. It is going to be really hard to find someone like you. I'm sorry I don't mean to overwhelm you…" I didn't immediately remember this part of my voice message earlier when I started writing that section. I apologize for not adding it in earlier and I admit, I did not want this to incriminate me! For months I felt guilty. Extremely guilty. I thought perhaps this was THE part that provoked him to block me. Almost as if he was trying to protect me from getting hurt. This is the reason why I had the ludicrous suspicion that he did what he did out of his own guilt and from a benign place of his heart. I thought perhaps he panicked because he never meant for that to happened. Or at least, it implies he actually does have a soul and did not want me to suffer. Of course my mind went here. Of course at the very beginning I actually thought he said "Mature up a bit" for this reason. That is precisely why I tried apologizing to him all this time thinking that is what he needed to hear in order to give me what I want—peace! That line of thinking is of course sadly only the "Hallmark" on steroids aspect of my brain speaking. This alternate universe is not within the realm of possibilities based upon what he said and HOW it came across and what he actually did to me beforehand and thereafter. The facts and his actions spoke for themselves and will continue to speak for themselves. I gave him MANY chances to redeem himself. He failed. Despite what I said in my voice message, it was entirely possible and

NOT so hard to offer someone like me in that moment an apology and explanation before blocking me. I was under a very specific impression, and I was experiencing a very distinct reality from what was actually the truth. I can not begin to tell you how ridiculous those words in my voice message now sound. I can not begin to describe the nauseating regret and disbelief I feel when I revisit those words and those emotions. He absolutely did NOT deserve any of it. But it was too late at that time. I felt what I felt and I experienced what I experienced. He had the power to change my fate by acknowledging me as a *person* who respected him so much and as a *woman* who loved him and desired him very much. I was incredibly fragile in that moment, and he increased that sensation of vulnerability by ignoring me all those months. I desperately needed closure and to *end my experience with him in good terms*. My pain was subsequently undermined and mocked so ruthlessly and mercilessly. Nothing justifies his cruelty towards me, and nothing justifies what unraveled thereafter due to his negligence.

Ladies and gentlemen, there is only one *Reality*. And it is very much fucked up and disjointed.

2. Scattered Glass

To reiterate, my name is Bride of the Rain on Facebook. Just call me Tasrit. It is written in Tamazight, the indigenous language of North Africa including Morocco where he is originally from. It is spoken by the Amazigh people. No, that is not a typo. People confuse "amazing" and "Amazigh" all the time. They are truly amazing people, and despite the events that unfolded with me and this individual, I hold no contempt for this community as they are like my own family. Him and I were not Tinder matches. We were not random strangers. The reality is we were part of a close-knit community on Facebook that focused on his cultural customs and on activism for the linguistic rights of his people. I taught myself his native language Tamazight, alongside Moroccan Arabic (Darija) ages ago. I have a good amount of followers from the Amazigh North African community because they considered my abilities really unique and cool. They welcomed me with opened arms, and I have never felt more at home. I can sing in the different variants of Tamazight too, and I do some regional dances as well. I may not always have the best technique, but I have a lot of passion for this topic. This is greatly due to the fact that I ended up discovering that I myself have Jewish origins from this region. I did not grow up knowing this information. However with the help of DNA tests and genealogical research and what not, I was able to reconnect with even some distant cousins from Morocco, Algeria and Tunisia. My mother is about 40% Moroccan and Algerian (Jewish) and even my father reaches about 15% Southern Moroccan Amazigh and Eastern Algerian specifically (he is also of Sephardic Jewish descent) with both parents having actual

33

North African cousins as DNA matches on MyHeritage for example.

Brahim Yaroud is his name and I knew him as Yugerthen Yaroud on Facebook. He and I had hundreds of friends in common. We knew each other for years. There is a specific reason he needed to meet me, and in my mind it had to do with this topic. That is my point. Where is the logic of wanting to meet someone all these years who has this kind of a respect for your culture and who you met under specific circumstances for the sole reason of having sex? Uhm... Okay... I am not insinuating he needed to fall in love with me. But I am insinuating he wanted my attention for *specific reasons*. He wanted *my affection* for specific reasons. He wanted to experience *me for who I am*. Otherwise why out of ALL of the women he could have fucked and cheated on his wife on that particular weekend, why did he have to choose me? So it begs the question why treat me like I was just a figment of his imagination so easily?

Yes of course this shameless piece of work was married. For 15 years exactly. He married a beautiful white woman form New Jersey. Mind you, at that time I actually thought of her as really beautiful. I am not being sarcastic I swear. I recall reading her "About me" section a couple of days after I came back from New Jersey. I remember reading "in a relationship since 2010." I did not want to believe it. I could not process this automatically. I had A REALLY hard time understanding that information. It unfortunately did not make any sense to me at that time, and I consequently suppressed any possible implications. I did not want to believe yet again another man (and specifically North African unfortunately) tricked or betrayed me. It did not automatically dawn on me that he could have been married.

But please hear me out here for a bit! There is a specific "Married" status on Facebook. Why not use it? Why cheat so openly with someone within his list of Facebook friends? I interacted with Brahim all that time on his profile while Nahara also simultaneously would interact or react to those same posts. Why did he take that risk knowing fully well I would end up seeing all of this publicly? That is extremely bizarre. Wouldn't you all agree? I never once saw a photo of them together on his profile. All these years this man interacted with people and especially with me as if he were single. That is probably the most compelling piece of this fucked up puzzle that made me doubt the legitimacy of their relationship, and furthermore that made me doubt he actually cheated. I hope that makes sense? Here's another piece of that same puzzle: I asked him that night if he has ever been in love. He said no! HE SAID NO! He told me the last time he felt something very close to love was with a girl back home in Morocco when he was younger in his 20's. He said that so confidently. Like he meant it. Did he assume I knew he was married and just assumed I'd be okay with him cheating on his wife? That is an insane assumption if that is the truth. Then why did he somewhat act a little suspicious that day when we planned to meet? He works as a TSA agent at the Newark Airport in NJ. He told me he worked that day, so I needed to wait for him there until he finished his shift. For some context, the man I met on the dating app came from a strict Afghan religious community and for personal reasons, he could no longer stay with me in New Jersey that weekend. That meant I did not have a place to stay that night. I ran out of money too. That is why I had to ask for help on Facebook. In regards to the Afghan guy and that part of the story, it sounds really strange I know. But there is a complicated context I am leaving out for the purpose of simplicity and staying on topic. So, why did Brahim tell me to meet him at a bar not so nearby instead? Why could we not leave from the airport? He said it had something to do with parking. It felt like he did not want to be seen with me in public? From that bar he took me to the Robert Treat Hotel nearby the airport. I wondered if he actually used his own name to purchase the room. I called the hotel and neither his name nor my name were on file. So did he use a different name? Clerical error perhaps? Fuck, I don't know! Don't we need to give out our last names with our room number in order to check out? I am pretty sure I did. I usually always keep the room keys just for fun! This one in particular I definitely got rid of when I found it in my bag for the sake of not keeping bad memories around! DARN IT! But still, didn't he think ahead? The room number alone is sufficient to look up reservations. So did he or did he not take precautions in order for her not to find out? Did he take all of these precautions earlier so that I wouldn't find out he was married? But then why hide your relationship status? His status was not even visible when we hooked up, and he immediately set it back to public when I came back from the trip. Why would he do all of that if he knew I was going to notice everything on Facebook? How could he not think about how that would make me feel? Did it not occur to him that I could have messaged her instantly to clarify who she was to him? Did it not occur to him I could have told her immediately what happened between us? Did he know I would be that much in shock I would not be able to say anything to her? All of this is just beyond insane! I also remember vividly Nahara had set her status to "It's Complicated" a week before I sent him my seven-minute voice message. (I admit, I took a screenshot of that!) It was during his trip to Morocco. I remember around that time period his relationship status was actually not visible *yet again*. And it remained that way for months up until early October of this year 2024. At that time in January, I started to speculate if that gesture meant they were indeed in some sort of complicated, on and off, or open relationship. I had imagined therefore, perhaps... they were on a break during the time we hooked up? That still doesn't make it ANY better. What a magical coincidence that would have been! So I am not buying that "break" theory. Why then would Brahim allow me to flirt with him or waste his time and my time in that fashion? Why? Did I forget to mention I yet again messaged him around late August? (Yeah..yeah I know! I KNOW! But please give a me a break! I have NEVER been hurt in this manner before!) Let me tell you what it means to be mixed with all sorts of Mediterranean populations. We are incredibly stubborn people. And speaking for myself in particular, I definitely have an explosive cocktail of "warrior" genes if you will! My pride and ego were left shattered for months, and for months I suffered dire consequences with my mental health. So yes, I REALLY needed him to apologize to me and offer me the explanation that I deserved! Yet I naively again began with apologizing to him in those messages. I was apologizing for my choice of words and tone I used during our argument once again. I was apologizing for aggravating him so much. I apologized for all the messages I was sending him. I apologized again if I judged him unfairly! I sincerely thought that maybe if I had spoken to him differently he would have reacted differently? I was honestly extremely out of it, livid, and pissed off at the fact that he blocked me back in July like I was some pest that he needed to get rid of. I was furious when I saw him heart react to Thasrith's display picture of herself and her cat. I was incredibly jealous and scorned. I admit, I was also incredibly jealous of Nahara. I was jealous of them both. I allowed myself to feel this way for the longest time because I wanted to hang on to the idea that there was possibly a misunderstanding. I was hoping their relationship was not what it seemed. I did not want to accept the reality that he cheated on her with me that night. Using my mother's account that she had deactivated last year, I sent him my very last friend request to be able to get his attention. (Yes, you heard me—this was the LAST time I tried to get his attention in that manner I swear on the life of my cats!) He ultimately gave up on blocking me and simply rejected the request and allowed me to go on and on with my messages (leaving them in that infamous other or restricted inbox maybe). Aww… how thoughtful of him! At the end of it all, I told him the things I should have told him from the very beginning. I will just leave it at that for now. I then finally gave in to the urge I have been fighting all these months to contact Nahara! I asked her what I was dying to know at that time! Did he or did he not cheat?

The answer she gave me was an obvious fucking YES!

I had no knowledge of him being a married man otherwise. And I had no reassurance of him actually cheating had I not contacted her. Yugerthen, married? What the actual fuck? This man is 41. And she is 54. He has no pictures of her on his profile. He has no pictures of them together, hugging or kissing or anything of that sort. All of their memories and photos of them together are in HER profile, and the photos that are there aren't so touchy touchy as husband and wife. He hides his relationship status from time to time. He would look at my pictures and stories all these years and he shamelessly and effortlessly proposed I could meet up with him if I visited his area years ago! He then shamelessly and effortlessly decided on his own to meet up with me last year.

Ergo, I was definitely *on his radar* or on his mind somehow! And of course as we all know, he shamelessly and effortlessly accepted my request in December of 2023 to hook up with me again if I visited NJ or NY. He is extremely flirtatious beyond control. I know how that sounds. We all know how that sounds. The optics of this relationship considering the facts are not good!

She did not take my point well AT ALL…

To explain, I messaged her with a spear in my heart and heavy palpitations in late September of 2024. I unsent that message immediately out of fear and out of an overwhelming sensation of anxiety. I had a feeling she did indeed notice the original "unsent" message, but she decided to shrug it off perhaps? We all know Facebook displays the deleted text as "unsent." Then suddenly, she decided to pay attention to me because I noticed she "liked" one of my public posts not too long after. I took that as some sort of a sign. I REALLY needed her to know what happened. I was being honest when I told her that I have been stopping myself over and over from contacting her because if I did it impulsively, that would have been more so out of revenge. I didn't want to be selfish. I wanted to make sure that I was thinking about HER. Keep that line in mind PLEASE! I wanted to make it clear to her that this time I have been losing sleep over not knowing the truth, and over the possibility of her going through an injustice. I told her this in a series of different voice messages. In my first and second voice messages, I told her the entire story, and I asked her for clarification on their relationship. "He has been my husband since 2011!" She said. "I am sorry you have been another victim." "This is just what men do. Some men just have a dark side!"

For fuck sakes. "Another victim" she said? "This is what men do??" "Dark side?"

You don't say…………………..

In the beginning, she seemed to take my side. I had to tell her even *very specific intimate things about myself.*

I told her about my PTSD and mental health issues.

Why?

Well, I told him the same thing that night in the hotel room. As I mentioned earlier in this book, I did not automatically start undressing myself in front of him. I sat on the hotel bed while he sat in front of me on a chair. We talked for a good 30 minutes or so. We talked specifically about my experience overall being in Morocco, and how much I loved being there. I told him how beautiful it was to encounter my friends who have supported me all these years in the projects that I have been doing. We talked about my involvement in helping some political prisoners from the Northern Rif region, be it by writing letters to organizations or through my essays as a college student. I talked about my encounters with famous singers from that region too. He knew I was associated with many well known people from his country. He even asked about my cat and told me I had a *beautiful cat*! (No—that's not a *double entendre*, I actually do have a beautiful white cat with blue eyes named Tanit after the Goddess of fertility of Carthage.) He seemed so normal and harmless at that time. We then finally talked about my previous marriages with North African men. My most recent ex-husband in particular was from Libya, and he told me that all these years he noticed I indeed had a specific type. He noticed the men I was married to. He had these specific memories of me. How interesting. What he never noticed or knew in detail however was how my ex-husband would verbally and physically abuse me. I would occasionally post about my experience with him on Facebook. Point being, I did mention in vague terms how much I suffered with my ex during that conversation with him in the hotel room. This is how the conversation led to me talking about my struggles with PTSD, Post Traumatic Stress Disorder. This information was meant to emphasize to Nahara that I was not someone completely random that he met at some bar. And yet, I ended up getting treated like a cheap whore he just met that night without thinking how that could affect someone with my conditions. Please allow me to rewind a bit here and analyze that night even further: After I opened up to Brahim about my mental health challenges, he looked at me firmly and said, "It's good that you are at least honest with the men you are talking to when mentioning this." Take a wild guess what I said afterwards? "And it's good that you are at least honest with women about your intentions." He smirked at that comment. I was referring to him specifically stating that he does not like to feel "trapped." He said he needs to be in "different places" and always going somewhere as opposed to staying in the same place all the time (I interpreted that to mean as opposed to staying with the same person all the time too). He precisely elaborated on this notion after my "Have you ever been in love?" question, right after he had answered "No!" He interacted with me cool as a fucking cucumber as if he were a single man. We both praised one another and *rewarded each other* for our "openness" and "honesty." The day after I checked out of the hotel, he touched base with me as any man would after they spent the night with someone they *knew*. He said "hey" in a cheerful good afternoon sense and asked me how did I sleep last night. He then mentioned he woke up late around noon and then told me his plans to go

41

to work later on. He then wished me a good flight with a smilie emoji at the end. That was also the last time he sounded *really* happy with me and utilized a happy emoji in conversation. No nervousness, no remorse for cheating and yet his emotions seemed incredibly genuine in my perception. If this book doesn't get selected to showcase "dramatic irony" in some shape or form, I am going to be DEEPLY disappointed. Because what the actual fuck?

I told Nahara what his husband did to me in detail. I explained in detail how this experience provoked me to contemplate ending my own life. While many people especially men with his toxic personality type would be tempted to call this emotional blackmail, I would like to respond by a giant FUCK YOU to that. Suicidal ideation may not be the same as an attempt, but it is very much real and it is very much painful, and it can definitely turn into an elaborate plan. A person could easily act upon it if it gets to that unbearable point of no return. I told her that when Mr. Yaroud and I had our argument in January, I was not completely aware of his serious or committed relationship with her. I was severely confused, and I told her the reasons why. I made it clear to her that because of my argument with her stupid husband I wanted to walk out of my house and run straight into traffic that day he ended our friendship horribly. I told her that this is the result of trauma. I explained to her that he was my last straw! I told her I had enough! I had enough of enduring the same story and pattern with these kinds of men. He had the choice to stay away from me that night. He had the choice to actually think about his actions after telling him the information about my mental health challenges. But he decided to ignore that and take that extremely lightly. I explained all of this in detail to her. But she ended up turning her back on me at the very end because I mentioned their age gap. A remark that was absolutely NOT meant as an attack towards her AT ALL. What I had said in my voice message was the truth. He is a Moroccan man about 13 years younger than her with a *particular set of interests* and who is interested in very *particular* women. That wasn't even the main idea of the voice message. That comment was left for the end, and was only meant to highlight his millennial immature approach to women. It was NOT meant to highlight her own age, but it was apparently a major insecurity and trigger for her. Brahim for a fact shows more interest in women like Thasrith for example, (who is a gorgeous blonde Moroccan woman from Canada). Or in German woman with big boobs holding a cold glass of beer. Or should I say German prostitutes? She admitted herself the reason she had set her status to "It's Complicated" on Facebook is because she saw a website on his computer where he was soliciting German prostitutes before his trip to Morocco. That was ONLY a couple of days before I had sent my infamous seven-minute voice message to Brahim.

I told you…

I have *extremely* bad timing!

So she had admitted to me he caught him cheating before two years ago, and she has known him for about 15 years. How the hell could she be THAT blind to the reality of these kinds of men then? I do not take what I said back. I asked her if she knew what she signed up for the moment she decided to spend the rest of her life with someone like him. I am not even talking about him as in his cultural background, I am talking him being *him*. I do not need to be a licensed psychologist to know that this individual is definitely wired in a particular way to act recklessly and lack any remorse. Ergo, narcissist or

43

even sociopath. (The only reason why I would even think to hesitate to label him as a psychopath or sociopath is because he loves animals especially cats—unless that is also some sort of elaborate scheme to fool those around him!?) These words get thrown around so much that they start to lose their original meaning and value. Ladies please refrain from using the words "narcissist" and "psychopath" or "sociopath" so loosely towards men. Not all men deserve this title. Some men are arrogant. Some men are lazy. Some men are *slimy.* But other men "have a dark side." The kind that literally makes women actually say that as if it's nothing. So yes I mentioned *he is younger* than her. Yes it was relevant. I did not say what I said in order to diminished her worth as she proceeded to do with mine. I said what I said in order to prompt a very specific response from her. I had this strange feeling in my gut that she somehow knew who I was and knew about the hook up. I needed to expose the truth. At the same time, although this will sound somewhat fucked up because I am essentially almost....defending her husband by this statement: It is NOT possible to expect him to be monogamous. These men with his kind of personality and from his particular region of origin aren't wired that way. That is something that I had to learn and that I eventually accepted. So the reason behind me emphasizing this to her that day was because I thought she would have accepted it too. I honestly felt that deep down inside she knew what he has been doing behind her back, and she will always forgive him no matter what. I am telling you with the upmost honesty I never imagined she would end up twisting my words. I was still very much in shock, and I was therefore still trying to find a logical explanation for his actions. Ergo, that was my intention behind that remark! I understand that perhaps I sounded condescending towards her. Almost as if I were a parent reprimanding an innocent child who didn't know any better. I was angry with her. Not because I was jealous, not because I wanted her to be miserable, but because I felt she was extremely passive towards Brahim's actions and that scared me and INFURIATED ME to the core. Despite that, I wanted her to see she was more valuable than to be used by a devious man taking advantage of her ignorance! She could have retaliated in many other ways if she really felt offended by my tone. But she did NOT have to behave in the manner you will get to read and experience further on.

She claims to be some sort of "energy healer" on her Facebook profile. But instead of her healing ability to purge Brahim from the darkness that lurks inside of him, the opposite happened. She has been consumed by his evil bullshit, and she spewed that against me. She thought I wanted to steal her husband away and thought that was my motivation for telling her my story of that night and of what happened afterwards. She thought I was lying or wanted to cause trouble on purpose. She said I was a bearer of ill-will and chaos. "Go destroy someone else's marriage!" she said. Sure. The woman who is married to chaos is telling me that I am destruction? "You are a bearer of ill-will and chaos!" She stated! Nahara and I were NOT supposed to be enemies. We were not supposed to hate each other. She was not supposed to doubt me! And I was not supposed to resent her this much! Those two have no idea what I have been through. I did not deserve this kind of an outcome!

She ended up teaching me a very valuable lesson: You do not want to be suffering in silence under the guise of love like her. *Maskeena! Poor thing!* She thought I needed help? No thank you. I am way too smart for a therapist. You try explaining "structuralism" to them or mention Claude Levi Strauss or Emile Durkheim or Aristotle during a session to get to a point and they always look at me like deer in front of headlights in the middle of the Sahara Desert or something. I am much too "self-aware" for their knowledge and for their "help." And the only usage a psychiatrist would have for me are certain medications that otherwise a PCP would not be able to prescribe. No need. I have my own inner strength and creativity to get my end result. I pity her as much as she pities me. The moment Nahara finally became a reality to me was the moment my mind had so much clarity, but my spirit was consumed by so much rage. As you may remember from the beginning of my story, Brahim had MULTIPLE opportunities to tell me about her and to tell me to stop messaging him NICELY and POLITELY. But he deliberately chose not to say anything. He did not even bother mentioning her during our argument. Why? Why cause this much turmoil and confusion to me? Why did he turn me into the person I am right now? I struggled so much to let go of the idea of him precisely because he did not have the courage to tell me about his wife and that he *loved* his wife!

Dear, Yugerthen Yaroud—Fuck you very much.

Because of you I lost myself and my self worth. And because of that experience I had thoughts of death Mr. "World of Work and Trouble." You wouldn't last a day in my shoes. You do not know what struggle is. You do not know what real pain is. You do not know what trauma is or what it can do to the psyche. You take your health and sanity for granted. You take your life and world for granted. Nahara's brother committed suicide and that is the source of her trauma. I was graphically sexually abused as a kid and that is the source of my trauma. What is the source of YOUR trauma and suffering? I was bullied and even physically abused in school. I was treated like the freak of nature everywhere I went. I had to endure horrible moments of humiliation by so many people. People I trusted. I trusted her to understand my walk of life as I did instantly with hers. How could you treat your own wife who seems to love you very much like an idiot? How could you manipulate her to the point she would forget her own humanity and undermine my pain? She can't be all that evil. She learned that from you! You are a sick person. You are disgusting. How did I ever fall in love with someone like you? You both then conspired against me?

Why did you? Because you thought you can judge me over some silly videos I have made in the past where I laugh and dance? You thought that made me an easy target? It's called having an alter-ego. You and Nahara would know a thing or two about that! I was merely trying to cope with my dark reality. I am actually not that quirky all the time. You met me in person. You know how well-composed I can be. You know I am capable of being that smart sophisticated mellow young lady. How dare you judge me! Did I have a sign on my head that said "Mistreat her" or "Use Her?" My life is not a fucking cupcake on a fucking unicorn. I had to fight like hell to survive in this society where people constantly underestimate me, patronize me, and invalidate me all the fucking time due to me being…*me*. By older people AND by younger people. I am constantly between a wall and a sword. I am sure you know how that feels. Right? I am sure you know how it feels to be treated like shit by all kinds of people. Go mistreat a blonde whore with an enormous ego who thinks you are atrocious and weird. Go patronize that dumbass coworker who thinks he is better than you or makes fun of you because of your accent or country of origin. Go hate on that boss or supervisor that treats you like you will never amount to anything. But me? I harbored emotions for you that were the complete fucking opposite under the assumption that you were a single man. Why did I deserve that from you? I am sure you know how it feels to be double crossed and made into a fool. Why then do the same towards me? You are such a fucking hypocrite. I am in constant pain both mentally and physically. But when I met you, I felt like all that pain vanished and nothing else mattered. I felt like I could conquer my pain and relinquish all of my problems and past demons while with you. With you I felt safe and protected. And yet, you became part of that menacing chain of "others" who harbored so much hate and darkness towards me. I remember reading a particular post on your wall back from 2014 that said, "Never underestimate the power in these three things:

Love, Spirituality and Forgiveness." Really? Mr. Atheist here is quoting 1 Corinthians? All I wanted in return was kindness and an apology from you Mr. Love, Forgiveness and so called Spirituality! For someone who is so godless, it seems God is sure looking out for you. Because it seems you got away with everything and you got everything and *everyone* you wanted at the expensive of someone's happiness and sanity. Tell me what was my sin? What did I do to you all these years for me to deserve this kind of an outcome? I respected you young man. I found you extremely attractive all these years. I appreciated your friendship all these years. I took you seriously. I would laugh at your funny posts. I found you to be a really cool guy. I would find your political ideas spot on and insightful. I thought you were so inoffensive and intelligent. I was not a hologram behind a Facebook profile, and I was not a figment of your imagination that night. I was a real person. You were real to me. Was I real to you? Why treat me like I am the psycho obsessed with you and trick your wife into thinking that is the truth? Why be this evil? Why me? I am not obsessed with you. Fuck you. I am obsessed with my own pride and ego that were shattered unjustly. How could I have been something yet nothing all at once to you? How? If you really needed some tight pussy that night last year, you could have gone to Artie's on 1121 NJ-12 Frenchtown, NJ and picked up a blonde babe. You know, to make up for the fact that Thasrith probably rejected your offer to screw you that time she came to New York last year in August of 2023. So I was your second choice on the menu that weekend? I was that chubby Mediterranean woman you wanted to use as an experiment all these years? I just wanted ONE positive experience with a man. And that man was supposed to be you. I was in desperate need of at least ONE act of kindness from someone I actually felt attracted to passionately. I needed a positive experience and kindness from you from point A to point Z because I felt there was *mutual attraction, respect and admiration* between two friends or least two people *who knew each other.* Something that I have never felt before and it was something I felt for the very *first* time. With you, I learned what I actually like in men in terms of physical qualities. I like men with your skin color and facial characteristics. Is that so bad? I used to be weary of dating older men, but with you I realized that is actually my preference. Only I thought you were actually a mature and wise grown up man.

I fell in love with you genuinely—*Neeshan Neeshan!* I did not only day dream about another intimate physical encounter, I day dreamed about your warmth (or lack thereof?). Your glow (or lack of?). Your awkward smile. Your energy. I had nothing but pure emotions for you. And yet, I wasn't even a friend to you. I was your perfect vulnerable victim. You think I sound batshit crazy? How the fuck is any of this my fault? Did I deserve an outcome where I had to contact a suicide hotline for the FIRST time in my life TWICE in February and in March of 2024? "Mature up" huh? "Let me respect you" huh? Despite coming across as so crass and as a jerk, I still thought of you highly nonetheless. I still did not judge you and did not *reject* you nor *avoid* you as other women or simply other people would. I still gave you the *benefit of the doubt* and felt that you were simply *misunderstood*. Yet I am the one taken for granted? I am the one discarded? I am the one you used only as a one night free trial? I am the one who needs to grow up? Because I told you beautiful things that I never told anyone before? Because I loved you in humanity which meant that I did not want anything romantic from you, only kindness and respect, but you bestowed me with the exact opposite? I was worthy of a rough intro but I wasn't worthy of a kind exit? Not even a graceful goodbye, an innocent "I'm sorry?" Fuuuuck!!! You use your wife as an ATM machine and you screw women from all sorts of ethnicities on those trips she pays for as she openly admitted to me, and I am the one who needs to mature up? How and why did I even fall for someone so vile like you? End Letter.

Dear Nahara / Dr. Jacqueline Ruth Ruskin,

I am obsessed with you and your husband huh? FINE. YES! Let's just say I am obsessed! FINE! But you want to know what I am not? I am not a hypocrite. I am not that broken like you. I am not passive nor complacent. At least I am actually not that much of a masochist that enjoys a relationship with a *false sense of love and security*. I am also not a liar. I am not a cheater. I do not gaslight people. I do not walk all over people. You are in love with someone merciless, with someone who can't even love himself. You are in love with a *lost cause*. You are in love with someone so broken. He loved the gratification I gave him, but he didn't love *me*. He loves whatever gratification he gives you, but he doesn't actually love nor respect you. What a fool I have been to think he was capable of loving and respecting someone like me.

 End Letter.

Whoa! That felt good. It feels so fucking good to let off steam in writing. It would be better if I could actually yell all of this in their faces and not just in "imaginary" letters. It would feel so much better if I can actually confront them and see if they both have the guts to respond to my arguments. I want to know how they would respond to someone hurting very very much. You will notice I will occasionally add in more "letters" in between paragraphs. Throughout the year I would get on my computer and begin composing letters to these individuals. This helped me cope with my emotions so much. They were written at different points in time during this journey, so they represent different alter-egos or states of mind. Stating this in case many of you are confused.

In between those therapeutic letters, I would gather inspiration to write poetry of course. It wouldn't become part of the last chapter of this book if those literary works weren't significant. They too reflect many of my states of mind during this whole experience. They manifest innocence, or the complete opposite. They demonstrate my longing for closure and forgiveness, and the complete opposite as well. As the story unfolds, the reality gets darker. So do my poems.

"Masters of deception
Two sides of the same coin
You are made for one another
A match made in a narcissistic-masochist heaven.
Enjoy the feast of your sacrifice
Enjoy this Eid.
Piece by piece
The bottom he clearly enjoyed, my mind she destroyed.
Reduced to nothing by self-indulgent fools!"

3. The Broken Mirror

Plot twist: I am certain they live separately. The puzzle pieces keep getting better and better and the more information I learn, the closer I get to having the complete picture! Nope. I am just kidding. This piece of information just made everything worse and my labyrinth of speculations just more nauseating. I remember back in December 2023, I noticed on his Facebook page he had set his location to Hyde Park, New York. It was set to New Jersey before that. Somehow or somewhere I distinctively remember his page stated he had moved to that location around that time. The internet is an interesting place! All it takes is a simple google search of their full names and literally the first link is of a mat-uncontested divorce court case that was settled (closed) in 2021. Yes these two idiots are divorced. A simple google search also reveals several different addresses under both names but Jacqueline as the proprietor. This is where my imagination REALLY took a ride into "One Flew Over the Cuckoo's Nest" land. So here we have a young somewhat handsome Moroccan brown man that was married to an older rich white woman with an exotic fetish for the Middle East. If this doesn't scream cliché toxic "90-Day Fiancé" type of marriage I don't know what does. For those of us familiar with the Moroccan or North African male community, we all know and I must re-state this as emphasis: the optics of this kind of relationship is NOT GOOD!!! I wonder if that is the reason behind him deciding to not be so vocal or *open* about their relationship? Did he want to avoid this kind of a judgement by people? Yet somehow I highly doubt that. Surely the people that he has met in person had their own reservations on their relationship? Did he hide his true intentions that skillfully that he managed to fool everyone around him and everyone in his internet world? "I am very open," he told me. Yes, he was very open about his trips, what he enjoyed and what he liked to do on his free time. Did I mentioned what he responded when I asked him that night in the hotel room when was the last time he had sex? He said last week in Portugal, with a Portuguese woman! That is some lovely piece of information. But how the fuck was he open about his *relationship* with Dr. Jacqueline Ruth Ruskin or aka Nahara Ruskin? Yes, Nahara is her beautiful alter ego name she utilizes on social media, although Jacqueline Ruskin is her real name (interesting she didn't become Mrs. Yaroud!) So by relationship, I mean *love*. How did he show he *loved* her in public. How did he show he loved her TO ME? What a shameless individual. So did he get married to her as a plot to then divorce her to only get access to some of her property and wealth? Why do I say this? She had no problem sharing this piece of info with me: "He is in Aruba, a trip I basically paid for, but now his trip is getting ruined by me sending him your voice messages that you sent me a while ago!" "I pay for his lavish lifestyle." Yeah…uhm… if she managed to say something like this to a stranger (me) that must be quite the burden she was holding on to. It was clear to me she was expressing a resentment or insecurity or *a truth* she subconsciously needed to let out in the open. "This is what men do." She was referring to him sleeping around. The verbiage she used made it so apparent to me that she was aware about his particular hedonistic habits and that she has come into terms with it. Is that why Brahim did what he did to me so easily? She is an enabler. She enables his behavior and rewards him for his recklessness like a kid. Their relationship is so odd and disturbing. Uncontested divorce and yet they went back to being a couple? Heck, did they remarry? Holy shit, was Brahim the one who was about to divorce her, but somehow he managed to convince her exactly how he needed their relationship to work out if she wanted to remain married? So many possibilities! One facet of my imagination sees him as the stereotypical archetype of the *opportunistic* Moroccan man who takes advantage of the sweet innocent older white lady for her money. Does he really have her wrapped around his finger with his sophisticated gaslighting tactics and sophisticated lies? For fucks sakes how could I NOT think like this? THESE TWO FUCKING IDIOTS HAVE NO IDEA how much I FOUGHT tooth and nail to get this idea out of my fucking mind. I did not actually enjoy speculating this! I tried contacting this "beautiful man" (quoting her after she told me off) for MONTHS and months and months precisely because I did NOT want to believe he was this kind of a person. I precisely tried to get the truth out of him so that I can have some peace of mind. Remember, I could not handle feeling this much love for someone so

54

ruthless. I did not want to come to the realization that he used and cheated on someone who I thought was very vulnerable too. Getting his attention was extremely important for me to finally let this go! But since he did not give a shit about my suffering, I had to contact his pseudo-wife Nahara for help. She only made my perception of Brahim worse. And paradoxically at the end she tries to convince me that they mutually both love each other very much. Ladies and gentlemen come on! Surely it is SO FUCKING obvious as to why I now have this particular perception of reality of these two! Clearly, Nahara is a very wealthy woman. Ergo, it is no wonder why Brahim chose her as his wife and would do whatever it takes to keep on using her. Right? I am just getting started. Wait till you learn what happened exactly after our argument just before she decided to undermine my pain so viciously. She had the audacity to post a taunting picture of themselves together at a bar the day after our conversation. The caption said: "Date night with my man. Fantastic 80's band at a local bar called Artie's. I am a sweaty mess and so happy." They did not actually look *that* happy. But those smirks on their stupid faces, I would not be able to forget them. That post was intentional because she then deleted it or made it not visible to the public after I confronted her about it. (Yes, I took a screenshot of it!) It was incredibly obvious that picture was meant for me. He had the fucking audacity to viciously break my heart and end a friendship by telling me to "mature up and leave him alone," while his own stupid "wife" acted exactly like a child. The nitric acid keeps flowing…. The act of infidelity, playing games with my mind, the patronizing, the rejection, and then the crazy pseudo-wife who treated me like a psychotic liar added more nitric acid to my wounds by uploading this photo.

It shattered me completely…

That is what she wanted and she had her victory. Perhaps I should be saying, this is what *they* wanted and *they* had their victory?

Okay. They want to play games like children?

Let's play!

Stupid buck teeth bitch and her bald asshole of a "husband." She acts like a child. He acts like a child. I may also act like a child. We are all children of the fucking corn apparently! Adults with unresolved issues. CLEARLY! BUT CLEARLY, these two have issues WAAAY deeper than I thought! He was definitely behind that photo stunt and behind her nasty words towards me. I know it. And even if she came up with that all on her own, he didn't stop her. He was reckless. She was reckless. The crack in the mirror just got bigger. The dominos just kept falling rapidly and violently. Was he the mastermind behind that? Did he comply to that thinking I messaged her out of revenge? NOTHING could have been further from the truth. I actually told Nahara to FORGIVE Brahim when she said she was about to kick him out of her house! FUCK!!!

My innocent love and desire for Brahim is a mental illness she claims? It is an obsession that requires the help from a psychologist?

Okay, sure…

In the voice and accent of a famous British Islamic Shi'a scholar: "Let's discuss and dissect this issue even further!" Her husband did not forget about me in YEARS. He reached out TO ME in 2019, and he reached out TO ME last year WITHOUT HESITATION. And without hesitation, he accepted to meet up with me again. He was not just a Facebook friend, he was also my follower. He would look at my photos and stories all these years. Out of all the North African men, married or not, who could have messaged me years back and even recently, Brahim/Yugerthen Yaroud was the ONLY one to do so. And out of ALL the women he knows, I made it to at least his top five who he really wanted to meet and fuck at all costs. He chased me FIRST! Let that sink in! What a strange coincidence he ended up blocking me after she probably threatened to leave him when she caught him soliciting those prostitutes (or other Facebook friends who happen to be German?). All of this unfolding after he took a luxurious trip SHE "basically paid for." During our one and only conversation, she told me she was about to kick him out to a tiny apartment with his sister. She wanted me to know he lives with her, OR in one of her properties at least. It now makes sense to me why he had to block me back in January precisely around that time he realized he was about to *lose it all, not her herself.* He blocked me because I mentioned my feelings and that posed a threat to his current "lavish lifestyle." He had the opportunity to block me before. Why didn't he? It is not like he blocked me because he wanted to avoid the temptation of sleeping with me again. Right? And it is not like he blocked me to potentially avoid falling in love with me right? I know if he were to read that, he would react in "whatthefuckness." But hey, I know that can't be true. That line of thinking would *definitely* be delusional! Right? But he had the choice to actually be open about her on Facebook. He had the choice to openly show that he loves her. He had that choice years back and last year. He so BLATANTLY acts like he can't stand her and literally shows more attention and affection to other women (as he once did to me). He does NOT love her. If he did, he would have told me the reason behind blocking me is because he is married and loves his

57

wife! UHM HELLO—he would have not slept with me and LIED so shamelessly to me that night! He acts as if he is ashamed of her. Yet I am the one who is mentally ill?

Well well well… If he truly is the evil man that I think he is, and he managed to gaslight her so fucking well to actually convince her to treat me like a liar and spew that kind of hatred onto me, then the only ones truly mentally ill are Brahim and Nahara. "I love him and he loves me! He is good to me and good to my cats and everyone loves him!!"

He is good to her cats…

…..

She said at the end of our argument. Yes she did. Yes. She said that. I cant even…..

"Even if he cheated that is what marriage is about, working through things!"

Excuse me? UHM WHAT???

EVEN IF HE CHEATED??? Sooo…………!?

She admitted that I was right? What does that imply then? She is OK with her husband treating me like a dumb slut that he used for my tight lower orifice that he REALLY needed to enjoy for one night because he can not otherwise have that daily? And this is OK because he is a man and some men have a dark side and he was doing exactly what men do? She supports her husband in his psychotic sapiosexual quest for hookups with younger beautiful nerds like me as long as she is the one who gets to keep him officially and forever?

Okayyyyy Shekinah and Sarper! (Kudos to you if you understood the reference!) I see how it is! She is okay with "her man" sleeping with other women as long as he never leaves her? Even if that means his love isn't very orthodox? It must be the effect of the *curse of the 2500* then! "Out of all the women I slept with or continue to sleep with I will keep choosing YOU Nahara!" If Brahim were to say something like this, I think she would be content as long as she gets to keep him as if he were some exotic brown pet. Because apparently her self-esteem is THAT low she feels he is the only man who will ever be able to tolerate her and find her somewhat attractive? That is why she has no choice but to put up with him cheating? And his self-esteem is also THAT low he feels she is the only type of woman who would be able to tolerate his darkness and madness because he knows a woman like her would consider a man like him *extremely* attractive and irresistible? Making it a lot easier to manipulate her? So they both decided to settle? What does she get out of this kind of relationship if Brahim finds other women more sexually attractive than her? A companion to drag him along with other old white people to "disco" nights? Drag Queen events? Don't get me wrong, I am absolutely NOT throwing shade to the LGBT community. But Brahim is the only straight Moroccan Amazigh man I have known to be interested in those things. It is very odd. Men from his background would usually not be in contact with disco music or queer events enough for them to consider partaking that much in those activities. That is my point. I remember many photos from those places. He would post those pictures at those places by himself however! Never did I ever imagine him attending those venues due to his wife Nahara! I wonder if he felt those outings were getting repetitive? I wonder if that is why he started to pay more attention to women like me? Those actually more interested in his culture or even those more closely connected to his culture? And yet their relationship has lasted for a good 15 years. Did he really just want someone to offer him a cozy home, (or different homes actually?) with home cooked meals in an environment where he can enjoy the beautiful canvass of red, yellow, brown and green during the fall (as opposed to those dreadful sepia filtered environments he has visited around the world, or the intolerable ashy atmosphere of New York)? He sure did win the lottery with her didn't he? And did she just want someone "foreign" but also very much "anglophile" at the same time with a slight "exotic" accent? He was some sort of proxy to Arab men that some American women go gaga for if you will? She wanted a younger exotic pseudo alpha-male who has an artificial "bad boy" vibe to make herself feel young, sexy and edgy? Do they even make love at all? It is strange how she did not mention that in our argument. Usually when a woman wants to prove a point that her husband loves her, she would usually boast about how many times they have sex with each other or in what manner. Does that make sense? So I understand I must have hit a DEEEP nerve with the age comment. Oops! But I DID NOT have the intention to offend her. My ASD brain can not shut off its impulsiveness sometimes and I do not always have a filter. That is NOT tantamount to having malicious intent. Yes, I am autistic. She was actually made aware of that in my voice messages to her that day. For those of you who may not know, people with Autism Spectrum Disorders experience the world very differently. Our senses are "heightened" and we process people and communication very differently. Autistic females are slightly different from autistic males. We are perceived to be much more empathetic and we *may* express empathy at higher levels than a neurotypical. We (may) also absorb the emotions of others at a greater frequency. We also mimic speech patterns from other people to come across as socially acceptable. She is from the east coast. I thought folks from her neck of the woods would appreciate directness? I swear to God that was actually my line of thinking. I thought she would know a thing or two about being neurodivergent. She acts like it honestly and dresses like a cartoon character sometimes—or as if Etsy vomited all over her. (Don't get me wrong, it takes one to know one after all!) Or is that just her neurotypical looney Gen-X self? Yes, I am having a lot fun here. FOR A REASON! Because to clarify ONCE MORE: I mentioned the age gap NOT to make her feel like an old hag unworthy of being loved by a younger man, but because I was just trying to figure out if what Brahim did with me actually counted as an act of infidelity or not. Do the dots connect? No? Okay, so my brain in that moment was in "get to the point" mode. So, I courageously presented the assumption that Nahara was made aware of Brahim's habits and thus be innocent from cheating IF in fact she allowed him to do so. Or at least, I thought she allows him to do so only because she herself has resigned from even trying to negotiate with someone like him. I made that assumption based on *different* variables.

Among those variables were: 1. His personality type, 2. The reputation men from his background have, 3. His reputation on Facebook based on my memories, 4. His reputation based on a conversation I had with someone who knows him and for all intents and purposes I decided to leave out of this book, and finally 5. Yes his age. I did not say "YOU are 13 years older," I said "HE is 13 years younger." There is a HUGE difference. I made this about him, and not about her. I presented a prejudice yes, but against him NOT against her. In our conversation I remember EXACTLY how I sounded and my state of mind. I was in horrible shape. I asked about her feelings if she was crying or in pain. I was wondering how she was processing this. I did not want to hurt her. I just wanted her to know the truth! I have nothing to apologize for. I have nothing to be ashamed of. I stand by the facts and I stand by the logical implications of those fucking facts. I do not need validation from people, but for what is worth, yes even other women would definitely understand where I am coming from and would gladly say the same to Nahara. What is sad is the fact that other women would treat her like a dumbass and not say anything. Other women would have not suffered thinking about her pain like I did. If in fact her husband denied our encounter and she believed him wholeheartedly, then that honestly and truly sends chills down my spine. That would imply him being absolutely ruthless and shameless to have control over her mind in that manner. That would imply him being THAT calculating and devious he is therefore indeed a man without a conscious. What reason would I have to lie? What would I gain? Nothing! I precisely told her NOT to tell Brahim about our conversation. Meaning I was not interested in causing any trouble. I actually was still afraid he could retaliate and say more hurtful things to me. I approached her with a lot of fear. I feared his wrath and hurting her in return. But I had to do what I felt was right! "That takes a lot of courage!" She said! Yes. I had the courage to no longer care about what he could say to me, and I cared MORE about her dignity. And that makes me mentally ill? This man has no real concept of right or wrong. He has no moral compass. You have to be THAT lost in your sociopathy or psychopathy to take control of a woman's mind to that point and to cause so much pain in the lives of those who actually love you. And you have to be THAT psychologically broken from past traumatic events to be a woman that would allow herself to be humiliated and patronized THAT much AND also be capable

62

of GASLIGHTING other innocent women LIKE ME. I innocently fell in love. And I innocently confessed to Nahara. How was it not obvious to them both that because he did not set any BOUNDARIES from the very beginning and tell me that hookup was supposed to be a ONE TIME occurrence ONLY, he allowed my emotions to buildup. How could he not imagine a scenario where I would fall in love because of that buildup of emotions? How was he not prepared to tell me nicely that he changed his mind? How could he not see that coming himself? Did he not foresee me speaking with Nahara? Or what other inferences should I be making here in the absence of crucial information? Information that I was begging him to give me and information she could have offered me too! So I DO NOT apologize for the things I said, and for the things I will say. Fuck that. Especially when she ended up spewing her toxicity in vain. Yes, in vain. She treated me like some sort of a threat. I was definitely not her threat, and perhaps she knew that and rejoiced in the fact that Brahim treated me like trash! That is the source of my anger towards her. I did not give her any reasons for her to come to that conclusion. It was so fucking obvious that I did not fit the profile of "the other woman." I made it clear to her how fragile and insecure I was this whole time. I put my emotions and feelings and vulnerability on a fucking silver plater for her. I showed her my jugular vein. She devoured me whole. How would she like it if I rejoiced imagining the next time her husband decides to eagerly be all over a younger woman as opposed to her? I hope that happens, and I hope she will remember me when it does. Yes. She clearly hit my DEEP nerve now didn't she? The difference is she did it deliberately to hurt me. I DID NOT have that intention. I wish I could hit another nerve and ask her if she ever thought to consider that all those outings to the lake, concerts and vineyards and so on were only after fights? I know that from own experiences. Did it ever occur to her to research what "love bombing" is? I bet that picture where she and her so called husband are smiling half-hugging side by side in front of a waterfall was only after he fucked up. That was probably the year she caught him cheating. It was also around the same year they both filed for the uncontested divorced. That was the last time she posted a picture of that nature of them together and left it public. Interesting isn't it? "Even if he cheated" huh? As I contemplate this statement a million times it HAS to be obvious to me that Brahim did confess and apologized to her (out of convenience), but he sure did not care about apologizing to me and for the pain he caused me. No surprise there. My goodness. She unleashed a series of very dark possibilities in my head we should now change "pandora's box" to "Nahara's box." Did she possibly make everything up? Either she lied about Brahim and her relationship with him, or she is associated with someone really contorted. They both cynically wanted to mess with my mind because they felt that threatened by the truth? Allow me then to mess with their minds too at least for a bit!

Dear Nahara,

"The energy you put out into the world is the energy that will come back to you?" You actually said this to me? It never occurred to you that your comments and your photo stunt that day could have provoked me to kill myself? It sure made my suicidal ideation worse you evil bitch! The mere thought of being made into a fool by not just Brahim, but by a woman I thought was innocent drove me insane. I hope you go to hell and I hope your brother looking down on you from heaven will feel nothing but shame for you. Please take your "If you ever need help please call the suicide hotline at __" and shove it up your *takhna/ tuchas.* I can tell you to go fuck yourself all day long too because I am so pissed off at you as well. But I never underestimated your worth. I never thought less of you. I thought you were attractive. I easily saw how Brahim could see a woman like you attractive despite you being older. I defended you! I told myself and others how can he take such a remarkable talented dancer and successful woman like you for granted? I would constantly be baffled at his behavior for months and months! And for the longest time I could not figure out WHY HE WAS NOT IN LOVE WITH YOU! And this is how you repay me? By undermining my experience and my pain and gaslighting me to the core using my own mental health challenges against me? How disgustingly cynical of you to even mention that suicide hotline in the beginning plus the anecdote behind your own brother to only then treat me like a deranged liar! Did it not compute in your fucking brain that the man you called "beautiful" <u>was the man behind my mental health crisis?</u> You had access to his messages this whole time you claimed? Did you not see his messages where he invited me to see him last year? How about back in 2019? "Private investigator?" Oh sweetheart, you don't need a fucking private investigator. All you needed was to have a talk with a Moroccan woman and she would tell you the truth that you so desperately needed to hear! Unless that talk with me was all bullshit? Unless you only took my side in the beginning to give me a false sense of comfort? Do you have any idea how humiliated you also made me feel? Do you have any idea how vulnerable YOU also made me feel that day? Oh I am sorry, was I supposed to allow your stupid husband to make a fool out of you? Was I supposed to keep quiet and allow him to use you like a moronic MILF for your wealth? I didn't want you to feel this <u>same sensation of vulnerability</u> that I felt with him and others. I did not want you to feel the sensation of utter defeat and hopelessness like he made me feel. Yet you decided to twist my words and undermine my pain? *You snake!* You knew very well who I was didn't you? Very interesting how you set your status to "It's Complicated" over some *random* prostitutes. But you did not do the same for me, over someone he actually *knew*. I bet Brahim did confess and he apologized to you, but you sure as hell did not want him to apologize to me. That was ALL I wanted and EXPECTED for you to do! I NEEDED you to be on my side and end my pain that I DID NOT DESERVE. I needed him to apologize to me. You saw my messages as you admitted to me! You saw how much I was suffering and you did NOTHING to help me. You had the power to change my fate and do right by me so that I could finally close this *chapter and be able to breath again, feel human again, and have a reason to live again.* I remember I used this verbiage in my messages to him. You saw that Ms. Energy Healer, Animal Lover, Empath? Fuck you! You *dark empath!* You deliberately kept me from the closure and peace that I needed out of revenge. You hypocrite. You then had the cynical audacity to claim that I wanted revenge? *You bitter scorpion!*

End Letter.

Dear Brahim,

Nahara does NOT love you for who you are. She loves you for how you make her feel. She loves you as a last resort. Now isn't that ironic? Out of all the good looking and successful men I could have slept with and fallen in love with, I chose you! And this is how you repay me? She knows you for 15 years and she still does not actually know you. It only took me a couple of seconds to know what type of person you were. And I accepted you for who you were instantly. I knew you had ambitions and that you were always undermined for having those ambitions. I knew you struggled to get where you are now in life. I admired you for that. I knew you had hidden talents and hidden emotions. I knew you weren't much of a communicator. I knew you weren't so romantic nor emotional. But I know you try your best. **That is precisely why I kept apologizing.** That is precisely why I trusted you and I kept holding on to a shred of hope that you weren't so horrible. I know many men reading this would understand and appreciate my intention. I assumed you were innocent. I assumed positive intent first. Who does that? You thought of me as a child this whole time? Are you fucking insane? I sure wasn't childish when you looked into my eyes and felt that electrical rush to take off my clothing and start enjoying every part of me. I sure wasn't childish when you contemplated meeting me again. I sure wasn't childish to give you the boner Nahara couldn't give you apparently? The boner that the other "Bride of the Rain" from Canada would NEVER think about giving you. I bet I was the most beautiful and intelligent and successful and pure-hearted 31-year old you fucked with a body count lower than your IQ apparently. Perhaps you figured that be the case and you really wanted to experience a pseudo-virgin? Damn. I open my legs for you willingly and innocently and this is how you repay me? I am unworthy of respect by men like you because I became a slut? But I would also be unworthy of respect by men like you if I were to have rejected you. What the hell is wrong with you and with men like you? Who the fuck are you? I sure wasn't annoying or worthy of a fucking "GO AWAY" like some fucking flea when you were inside of me telling me how good it feels. You sure as hell did not tell me "GO FIND SOMEBODY IN YOUR TOWN" when I came to visit "your city" as you called it. You arrogant asshole! I sure as hell was worth your time and energy to thrust inside of me and yet, I wasn't worth your time and energy to be treated like a decent young lady who had nothing but pure intentions. Fuck you for actually attempting to gaslight me into thinking I was in the wrong. The only child here is YOU. YOU played a dangerous game with the wrong person. YOU do not get to treat a woman like me as a frivolous Facebook interaction without a heart, without a soul, without dignity, without pride and an ego and think you can get away with it. You thought I had a lane to abide by like a slave Brahim? If you actually managed to convince your stupid wife that I was a liar and a mentally deranged person, then you are officially one of the worst psychopaths, or sociopaths or narcissists to have ever been born out of Agadir, Morocco. You bring shame to your community, to your lineage and family. Did you deliberately choose a wife like her because she has a dark past like you, a weak personality and a malleable brain just to get a hold of her wealth? I tried believing in your innocence Brahim. I tried apologizing. I tried to believe in an alternate universe where you did what you did with no intention to hurt me. But the facts speak for themselves. The facts speak. And they will continue to speak. I know I sound like a lunatic to you and I do not give a flying fuck anymore. Even us lunatics deserve mercy and kindness and respect. You on the other hand are a soulless, insatiable, immoral lunatic who will never be truly happy and who will never find real success.

End Letter.

Other facets of my imagination has led me to even believe their relationship is just simply a façade for specific people to

68

see? Perhaps she is running away from someone and Brahim just wanted to help her? Then she fell in love and he can't leave her out of pity? Is this just your classic case of the 3rd world citizen needing proper entry into the U.S? And then they entered into some sort of an agreement to where he gets to enjoy her wealth as long as she also gets what she wants? (Whatever *that* may be…) What else am I supposed to think about someone who isn't transparent about his relationship status and who doesn't show he is proudly in love with his wife? Is this just your average classic tale of the bored married man who uses a poor innocent young lady (me) as an escape? To get his wife jealous? To get her angry because she made him upset first? But despite all of that he does indeed love her very much and tries his hardest not to cheat and hurt her. Although they had NO problem using someone innocent as their sacrificial lamb to save their marriage! Oh yeah, that doesn't sound fucked up at all! Instead of using your average New Jersey gal in her 20's from some bar or club to be able to achieve exactly what I just mentioned, let's use a young lady who you have known for almost eight years who is also very well known by your own Amazigh community here in the U.S AND by thousands of people in Morocco and Algeria—who came all the way from Texas and decided to meet up with you purely out of coincidence and who trusted you wholeheartedly just as a means to a very sticky white end! This is a Lifetime movie worthy plot I swear to God. I might consider turning this story into a movie one day! Someone please help me contact Ay Yapım (Turkish drama production company). I can not wait to see Alp Navruz or Melisa Aslı Pamuk as the main characters in this story! This is a if you know, you know situation. Google would be your best friend here. This is me still desperately trying to see the good in people. This is me still thinking highly of Brahim and Nahara because otherwise the reality of this entire situation is really THAT obscure? For the record, Alp Navruz is a thousand times more handsome than Brahim. I was being extremely generous there, but I actually do resemble Melisa Pamuk a little. Hazal Türesan can play Nahara. But if I were to actually chose a real life Turkish drama to represent my story it would definitely be "Aski-memnu," or "Forbidden Love" starring Beren Saat. In all fairness, this is how *I would have loved* to imagine my story with Brahim. Except it would be in the inverse. Brahim would be Bhiter and I would be Behlul for obvious reasons! Google would also be your best friend here to understand the reference. Haha! I am obviously just kidding. I needed to have that little bit of fun!

To Nahara/Dr. Jacqueline and Brahim/Yugerthen,

Miss so called vet at the Smith Ridge Veterinarian Center in NY and at the VCA Animal Healing Center in PA. Miss so called "Movie Star" in "The Dog Doc" documentary available on Amazon Prime! Please let's all ask her when is her next brunch date with Selena Gomez or Sydney Sweeney! But who is he? What reputation does he have? Who is Brahim related to that makes him feel soooo fucking special? He lives under HER shadow. SHE is the one with the career. He is the one with the 9-5 job. He aspires to be a Homeland Security agent. *Zaaama*!? Really? With what skills exactly when you can't even read people? Because if you did, you would have known NOT to make a woman who is already so insecure, fragile and emotional feel humiliated and betrayed so unjustly. You are so impulsive you do not know how to think ahead. Critical thinking skills anyone? Talk about Delusions of

Grandeur ladies and gentleman! I may also have one. I may have many. But at I least have the ovaries to admit it. Oops. Was that too harsh Mr. "I don't have time for this shit?" Not as harsh as you saying all of that to me after I had exalted you on a fucking throne of nauseating compliments. Not as harsh as you not willing to address my profound voice message that day. Not even with an apology and a fucking farewell! Nope, not as harsh as that! And what about you Ms. "Go destroy someone else's marriage?" Where the fuck is your humility? I don't see people in New Jersey or New York dying to have your autograph! Pipe Down! But people I did not know in Alhoceima and Nador sure did ask me for selfies when I was in Morocco. Let that sink in for the both of you.

Interesting. I don't have the accolades nor the money that you may have Nahara, but I had those beautiful Middle Eastern eyes that night that he absolutely lusted for with his own eyes. His pupils caressed mine. Those are seconds you will NEVER experience. Ouch. Did that hurt? Yeah, so did your sinister smile on that photo. So did your decision to abandon your so called intellect and fucking female intuition that day when you gaslighted me and mocked my pain.

End Letter.

"About to ride a horse so I can meet a nurse." This was a comment he left as a reply on a photo of him in 2015 wearing a cowboy hat. I vividly remember that photo. And I remember how much I felt attracted to him then. His countenance seemed normal and harmless. He looked happier then too. His reply was to a woman named Mazryah Taziri. (May her soul rest in peace.) She passed away from cancer a couple of months after he posted that photo. Mazryah was a very important person to me. She taught me everything I needed to know about her own Amazigh Shawi people of Eastern Algeria, about the history of Numidia, and the legendary Queen Dihya of that kingdom. She was a wizard with information, and she esteemed my passion for her culture very much. And I highlight this once more to emphasize the fact that Yugerthen and I shared a world together. A world that Nahara does not understand and one she was clearly oblivious to. His Facebook name, "Yugerthen" in fact alludes the one of the mighty rulers of Numidia. He ultimately brings shame to that prestigious name! I emphasize these details because he precisely felt what he felt for me, be it lust or a dark curiosity because of *this world.* At least a fragment of my mind told me so. Clearly to me he had his specific preferences in women. Clearly I am not his physical type at 100%. So in my mind, it made sense that *my knowledge* and *passion* for his cultural background contributed to him being that interested in me, he considered meeting me not once but *three* times. In 2019, last year in October and last year in December. But as I contemplate that comment section from 2015 with him and Mazryah, suddenly everything about my perception of reality towards who I *thought* he was and who I *think* he is starts to make… less sense. Nahara is a vet, she is not a nurse, so he was not referring to his own wife when he made this kind of a comment IN PUBLIC. Right? I wonder what she thought of this when she saw it. Then, after a couple of months of reading this section back, I had this odd yet glorious idea to perhaps google this phrase? I am not a fan of the show Yellowstone. It turns out it is a line from this show! Holy Shit! I really had no idea! He did not write that with quotation marks; it genuinely seemed like a phrase someone could easily come up with for a caption. But then again, maybe he is not *that* creative? Anywho, here is the catch: Mazryah (again may her soul rest in peace), had replied with: "*Wink Emoji*—You do not need to get hurt to meet a nurse or doctor." She obviously did not know what he said was a line from a show. But she flat out flirted with him. This woman was in her late 40's or maybe even close to 50's at that time. She had a nice body and soul. She was very beautiful. I dare to say she could have been his type even! Brahim flirted back by saying: "I will let my *horse* do the thinking about that Taziri!—*Smilie Emoji.*"

I will let you be the judge of all of that. To me honestly, I highly doubt he was talking about his own wife. Why hide the identity of someone you are supposed to love openly? Why speak in code like this? If she has access to his Facebook profile because she has his password, I wonder since when? If she had it since then, I really wonder what she thought of this entire conversation? Why use verbiage so openly like this if he were truly in love with her? If he were truly someone respectable and to be respected? You see, my memories with him were real and they were very meaningful and powerful. But I know they do not compare with memories you have with an actual person you experience physically with all your senses for years correct? And yet, without any hesitation he decided to sleep with me as opposed to his own wife that weekend. Very interesting. Yet I am the one who is delusional? I am the one hallucinating?

I also remember a picture he posted in 2014 that I saw in 2016 when he first added me on Facebook. It was during the Amazigh New Year celebration (Yennayer) in Boston, Massachusetts. There were members of a cultural association behind him holding the Amazigh flag, and Brahim was sitting down on the floor with his arms crossed. His fingers are freakishly long. His eyes were squinted and he looked high on crack. The comment section (or the comment section of that shared post) was hilarious indeed. I distinctively remember having a FaceTime or WhatsApp conversation with my other good Amazigh Moroccan friends from Ouarzazate. They were making fun of Brahim in that photo. They said he looked like a demon. It was all in good faith and everyone had a laugh. I remember I laughed too. I didn't think anything of it at that time, but perhaps that should have been my first warning?

It is incredibly tragic and sad that all these memories now are completely tarnished.

After Nahara and I had are first conversation, she ended up logging into his account and made his relationship status publicly visible again. (Only because I had mentioned the absurdity of him occasionally making it private or not part of his profile.) I still find that extremely suspicious. How on earth does she expect me to believe she has not noticed that? How pathetic it must be to force her "husband" to set that status as "Public" every time. It is REALLY hard to not come to the conclusion that she lied to me. She must know he does not actually love her and that he has never loved her. Right?

I posted public comments on her Facebook account. I did the things I should have done from the very beginning. I decided to not have fear anymore, and I demanded Nahara to tell his stupid husband that he needed to apologize to me. I told her that she may not care what he does to her BUT I CARE ABOUT MY OWN FUCKING PRIDE AND EGO. No, I did not actually say that exactly, I just like repeating that phrase over and over and in CAPS. It feels very liberating. What I actually posted were well written, well composed very much level-headed nice short essays in her comment section. (Nope…!) Everything imaginable, a combination of all the ideas I have expressed in this book—I made sure to let her know! I was like that video game character who had less than 10% of health (or down to two hearts) fighting till the last second to defeat the main boss in that epic final level. I needed to throw the last punch no matter how pathetic, how weak or how frantic I may have sounded. Anything I could do to disrupt their peace as they disrupted mine, I needed to do as well. There was nothing left for me to do other than that and finishing and publishing this damn (and very precious) book. Brahim made me feel completely powerless and vulnerable that day in January and up until now. Some people may continue to think I am crazy and wrong for holding on to my pride and ego in this manner. Are you also the stupid ones who believe in karma? (I'm sorry, but no offense.) Karma? What karma? I tried getting some sense of "justice" (in the most ridiculous sense possible) back in March of 2024 by convincing a mutual friend on Facebook to block him. In all honesty, I ended up doing him a favor. He blocked Yugerthen (Brahim) in a heartbeat. To that particular friend, "virtual friends" were meaningless. Interesting. No wonder those two were friends to begin with. Then a few months went by and that same so called "friend" who I had on my Facebook for 12 years (also from our so called close-knit North African community) ended up blocking me twice, on my main profile and on the second one I began to use when this whole journey started. He did this for reasons that are unknown. I of course did imagine if Yugerthen had anything to do with that. But that would honestly be truly bizarre. If this doesn't cause you to laugh hysterically, please reread what I just said. So I thought I could teach Brahim/Yugerthen a lesson by making him feel just a minuscule amount of confusion and shock when I found out I was blocked, if his friend that he had for a long time suddenly blocked him too. "Who gets blocked with the expectation of *eventually getting unblocked?"* Remember when I said this in the beginning? I had written that section way before that particular incident happened. Do I even need to say it? Do I? For the love of God!!! Beautiful irony. Beautiful. Right?

So…

How could I NOT felt so defeated? I felt that hopeless and vulnerable I just needed a minuscule amount of "justice" no matter how ridiculous that sounds. It is incredibly sad to know that his would definitely be considered childish to people like Brahim. They lack emotional intelligence. They lack intelligence in general. Attempting to seek revenge or "justice" is immature to him huh? The "an eye for an eye" mentality is immature? Retaliation is childish? But acting like a horny senior in high school who can't keep it inside his pants while acting recklessly as if life bestows and revokes, slows down and speeds up only at his whim is the epitome of supreme wisdom? Sure, we have already established that changing one's mind is only human. Making mistakes is only human. But my mistakes aren't worthy of forgiveness? I did everything to play nice with him but his ego truly has a ghoulish mind of its own. He might have decided to keep blocking me because of my decision to seek that form of retaliation. Can you believe I actually did feel remorse for something so innocent? Yes, I ended up apologizing for making that one friend block him. Oh Lord…Not only that..I actually told myself seeking that kind of innocent retaliation is what I needed to do in order to feel better and in order to AVOID messaging Nahara. I even mentioned that in one of my messages to Yugerthen/Brahim.

76

"Even if this is a misunderstanding and you didn't cheat, I am sure Nahara would not appreciate you causing this much psychological harm to someone innocent like me! That's because she is an empath like me!" In other words, I was fighting the urge to contact Nahara because I did not want to cause him or them any trouble, BUT I was warning him that my patience was running out, and it was running out VERY quickly. Take it as a threat, or warning I don't fucking care. The point is I was desperately trying to AVOID DOING THAT had he only been a fucking man and confront me with the truth! Oh the painful dark fucking irony....JESUS CHRIST.

I swear on the life of my cats this entire story is real!

"Look, I was not supposed to be your enemy. Please open your eyes. Have a heart! You knew DAMN well I did not approach you with the intention of hurting you...I said what I said because...." I essentially went back into her profile around late November 2024 to repeat what I mentioned earlier. My reasoning. My justification. I also desperately wanted her to be on my side and do right by me. I had decided to just shut up. But... Uhm—well you know! I gave her my last three-paragraph comment on her public profile as if I were entering that last dungeon with only 5% health or stamina (down to only one heart), zero magic on your meter, and with no elixirs nor special weapons to help you fight and defeat the final boss. Sadly, I knew it would be futile. She finally decided to make her profile visible only to those who know her, and she blocked the profile I chose to post a bunch of comments. What did I expect right? I thought maybe I could finally get her to come to her senses. I thought maybe Yugerthen/Brahim could finally realize what was happening and offer me the apology I was longing for. Nope. Game Over. He got away with everything. I ended up getting blocked by a man I truly loved and that I innocently desired. I ended up getting treated like a mentally deranged slut. I was made a fool of and I was belittled in the most vicious way possible by two fucked up individuals. I was patronized to the core and I was expected to remain passive to it all!

I imagine myself right now in front of him. And all I can see is a mirror. And what is reflected is anything but beautiful and special. I see someone ugly and unworthy of love and unworthy of desire. I see someone fragile and frivolous. I see someone ignorant and very much unintelligent. I see scraps and leftovers. I don't see someone worthy of life and living and I don't see someone happy. He gave me this reflection when I think about myself vis-à-vis my interest in him. And he has made me believe this is exactly how he sees me. How unfair. I fell in love with every inch of his body and of his soul. I fell in love with his deep gaze and eerie countenance. I fell in love with his voice and weird mannerisms that I deeply, deeply miss. I fell in love with his thoughts and his worldview. I loved him for his past and for his present and I wanted him to be my future. I fell in love with his shyness and his awkwardness. I can remember feeling so magnetized to him when I contemplated a specific photo he posted on Facebook. He was wearing a black T-Shirt with his Amazigh "Aza" necklace. (This is the letter Z in the Amazigh Alphabet called Tifinagh.) He was precisely on his trip to Germany when he took this photo. Meaning he was probably on his way to fuck German prostitutes or had already done so. Yet the cynical irony is that I remember contemplating this photo as if he were single and as an innocent inoffensive person just enjoying his stay in the land of schnitzels and cold jugs of beer about to "ride a horse so he can meet a German nurse or a Portuguese tourist." Never did I once looked at that particular photo or any photo involving his trips imagining he was actually cheating on his wife and making a complete fool out of her. Never did I once look at his photos imagining all of this would one day happen. There was something about the look in his eyes in that photo that sent electricity up my veins. Yup, I fell in love with his darkness just like Nahara. But it was clearly a trap. An illusion. It is an illusion that I deeply miss no matter how fucked up that sounds. He was never real, the *he* of my mind. But whoever he was in my memory, I will forever deeply love and deeply desire and deeply miss. I will never regret meeting *him.* But the man I know he is *now,* the Brahim in reality—I despise deeply. I fear him, I resent him, I loathe him, I pity him—I wish I never met him. Nothing I did changed anything. Not the messages, not my posts or videos about this on Facebook. Nothing! The only thing I get out of this is imaginary justice from an imaginary friendship and love.

And yet he never knew that he was my *first real* love.

My *first real* heartbreak. My *first real* deception.

The most powerful fragment of my memory to fuck me up so terribly. He was not *that* unique I suppose. He was not *that* special. He was not different from the rest. And yet paradoxically, he became my most unique and very special experience. He was definitely the "stress crack" in my emotional fragile labyrinth of crystal dominos that I needed to finally realize that there is a serious problem with my current perception of love. I need to have more self-respect. I need to have more strength. I need to stop being so weak. But I am never going to stop being me either. I battle between reminiscing and regretting. But now I realize I need to utilize those sweet memories as a criterion. I need to extract what I found attractive and disassociate from what is harmful. "I had a deep conversation with Brahim, what happened made our union stronger. I hope you find a loving relationship so you can stop meeting strange men and put yourself in harms way. You will never find fulfillment in doing so!" Signed, Nahara. Aww. Thank you for the advice. First of all, we have already established Brahim and I weren't strangers. And furthermore, she is admitting that he has an element of danger huh? And I thought I was the sad masochist who was unreasonably stubborn! I should write a poem inspired by this and call it "Sadistic Love." Sounds like the perfect title for that Turkish drama that will one day be made inspired by my life! I found my fulfillment in realizing I am better than you both. He gave me that gift, and she added the crimson red ribbon on top to seal the deal. Inside that box was the forbidden fruit I needed to taste in order to acquire supreme knowledge and wisdom of myself and of the world. I have been approaching men as if I were walking on a mine field since my relationship with my ex-husband, but now he has officially laid out new rules to that same mine field. Rules I will engrave in my mind, body and spirit from now on.

4. Shards of Evil

"But why Zelda?" "What was the root cause?" "What exactly led you to feel this way so intensely?" People may ask. If it wasn't already obvious or clear, the issue was never about Brahim reciprocating my feelings. The root issue is not about love. It is about a lack of respect, blatant lack of remorse and kindness. It even goes beyond the infidelity itself. It is truly due to the unique and bizarre nature of this story. It is about something *spiritually deeper*. I was humiliated and taken for granted. I was only taken serious for one thing only. And when I spoke about painful realizations earlier, it ultimately also comes down to him undermining me sexually. Will you have the patience to understand these profound concepts?

Let me explain: In the movie *"The Butterfly Effect"* with Austen Kutcher, there is a graphic scene involving abuse among children. Please either read between the lines or research the scene online. Does that not create some sort of a visceral effect in your psyche? This is the sensation of vulnerability I have been trying to explain. The movie also brilliantly explains the concept of a chain reaction on the basis of *minor* actions or choices made. It is in the title. The flapping of a tiny butterfly wing has the power to bring upon a storm. That is the analogy of my life, and that is what led me to experience what I explained in this book. This book itself is testament to that concept. When I was sexually abused as a child, no one was there to help nor protect me. No one was there to help me nor protect me from other acts of violence or psychological distress that I would then experience thereafter when I got older. Ergo, I have a very strong visceral reaction to vulnerability and its *co-infections*. You see how "self-ware" I am? I don't need a therapist or therapy session. I needed justice, redemption and validation. I needed closure, peace and *reciprocated remorse*. I needed an explanation, and the truth. I needed a sincere apology. I needed kindness and respect. Now I just need this book to be read and shared and understood. I have encountered people who would undermine my trauma either by not believing me or not taking me seriously simply because "it happened a long time ago." This makes me feel even more vulnerable and hopeless every time as if the *event itself is happening again*—that is the result of trauma/PTSD. That person who harmed me is a member of my own so called family and is still relevant in the lives of my parents for example. How could it not matter? 9/11 was a long time ago and this country is still involved with Israel/Palestine and Iran as a direct result of that event that jumpstarted a *new chain reaction* from an *underlying issue that was already in existence.* Brahim therefore flicked the first domino in that new chain reaction the moment he proposed that we could meet up with each other if I were to visit his area back in 2019. It then gain momentum when he decided to sleep with me last year while being in a relationship with someone else. He failed to understand the psychological and emotional consequences to implicating me in an infidelity. The dominos kept falling one by one as my emotions kept building up because he allowed me to feel this way and allowed me to interact with him on Facebook as if we weren't doing anything wrong. We were potentially about to meet up again behind Nahara's back. And I would have been just as confused and blinded by that reality if that were to have happened. I became infatuated with him. I fell in love with him intensely. I could not let go of our first memory together. I needed this experience to have a happy ending. My intention was to only have one more night together at least, or potentially keep things casual between us. I really wanted to continue experiencing him! And again let me restate this, me feeling this way is a <u>DIRECT</u> result of his choices. I showed him humility and insecurity. That was me already being vulnerable towards him. I exposed my jugular vein the moment I exposed something else to him. People can say I was also careless and I should have listened to my initial intuition. But I was not the one in a relationship. I am human, and I decided to give him a chance and not automatically assume he was dangerous. I can also blame myself in this situation. But on the other hand, I was doing something any woman in my position would do. I have the right to practice my sexual freedom in this country, so I was not doing anything illegal. I have the right to enjoy a simple hookup. I had the right to fall in love with someone I thought was good and available. I therefore had every right to experience that amount of confusion and dismay when I started to realize the truth little by little. He ultimately introduced me to that same sensation of vulnerability I have known all my life into this new chain reaction of events unfolding very quickly yet very slowly at the same time. Perplexing. I did not expect him to block me after my voice message that day. That was definitely tantamount to a slap in the face or slamming the door in someone's face. I am right. He was wrong. No one will ever be able to change my mind. Nothing justifies his actions from the moment he met Nahara, till the moment he met me in 2016, from the moment he began the first chain of reactions in 2019, till the moment he slept with me last year, from the moment he allowed me to flirt with him, till the moment he agreed to sleep with me again, from the moment he blocked me in a blink of an eye, till the moment he spoke to me horribly, from the moment he rejected me, till the moment I realized he prefers women like the beautiful Thasrith instead of women like me, from the moment he kept blocking my other messages begging him for an explanation and for closure, till the moment he kept interacting with Thasrith and Nahara as if I never existed. (For the record, I am not trying to antagonize Thasrith. She and I have been Facebook friends also since 2016. It is really sad that I ended up feeling so jealous of her. I offer an apology if she ever gets to read this book. I am not putting her on the spot as a villain. I did attempt to message

83

her to see if she and Brahim managed to *you know* together. I needed that piece of information to help me with my situation with Nahara! I felt she let me down. I felt she took me for granted too. As a result, I sadly had to block her. She is being used in this book symbolically more than literally. That being said, it is the honest truth based on my observations and on female intuition that Brahim feels really attracted to her.) That must have been the worst part of this whole experience. Realizing that the reason behind him blocking me and ending our "friendship" was not because he was in love with his wife, but rather because he would rather be intimate with someone much more desirable to him than I. That was the part that drove me completely insane. Why? Do I really need to elaborate what *rejection* could do to my kind of brain chemistry? I know what I am about to say might sound incredibly fucked up, but we are honestly past that point. If he was going to have sex with other women anyway why not with me? Yes, I guess my argument with Nahara made it incredibly easier for me to think this way. BUT I thought this way BEFORE, only because I was convinced he was not in love with anyone much less married to anyone! That was his fault for allowing me to think this way. I know if I were anybody else truly embodying what he considers as his object of desire, he would ask that woman to have an affair with him. It is not that I would actually do that outside of this dark hypothetical, I just feel incredibly humiliated at the fact that other women would actually be worth the trouble and I was meant for.....? A cheap thrill? I am not everyone's cup of tea. BUT HE ISN'T EVERY WOMAN'S CUP OF TEA EITHER! He is funny looking. He has a potato shaped head, he is 5'8-ish and he has this creepy look in his eyes at times. Honestly, how the fuck would he consider me beneath him or under his league? If he was my favorite cup of *attay, w*hy wasn't I then deserving of a *gentle, humane rejection*? Ah! Because I was not his <u>ultimate object of desire.</u> Fuck! That realization itself, the moment it was clear to me the "Bride of the Rain" he preferred was not me, but the other one who lives in Canada, was exactly the realization that made me not want to exist anymore. I felt so vulnerable it felt like someone was slowly suffocating me until I could not longer think for myself and until I could no longer breathe. As if you are vivid dreaming or having an episode of sleep paralysis and you can not move nor talk while you are aware that you are dreaming. You therefore end up feeling that sensation of utter panic and distress! I understand men have their preferences. But then <u>why *deviate*</u> from what you desire and trick an innocent young lady into thinking she is important to you? He did not have to treat me like a last resort. I was not scraps. I was not leftovers. Nahara may not mind being treated like breadcrumbs, but I DO MIND. He made me feel extremely *ostracized* and worthless. This entire experience from point A to Z has been extremely humiliating to my soul. I experienced all those emotions in the beginning under a *very* specific state of mind where I believed he was single. And he continued to act as if he were single and showed me he didn't actually love his wife. It created a lot of confusion. If it was not already clear to you, the incident after speaking with Nahara created the *last phase of this domino effect.* I was indeed on the verge of entering <u>my first phase of healing</u> from this experience albeit in a very slow manner, but she fucked up. I just finished explaining how vulnerable I felt vis-à-vis Thasrith and Brahim, imagine then feeling utterly confused and hopeless when it came to thinking about Nahara. If Brahim shows this much excitement to a woman like Thasrith, why be married with Nahara? What is her purpose in his life if he treats her so condescendingly? THAT was my motivation for contacting her. And now consider what just happened between us! If only she had convinced Brahim to apologize to me and NOT upload that photo on her profile of them laughing at me in their victory celebration date, this book would have been written VERY differently, and most importantly I would have not been in this current state of mind where I now do want revenge. Why put someone innocent like me in this position? From the moment she decided to not believe me and undermine my pain, till the last words of this sentence, I have not been able to fight back this agonizing sensation of vulnerability and hopelessness that he triggered in the first place. I must repeat for those of you who think I am exaggerating—I was slowly trying to *heal* from all of those past experiences I endured UNTIL I encountered Brahim and his wife. I have been ridiculed all my life. Belittled. I have felt meaningless by so many people. I was made fun of for the way I talk, walk , look and even dress. And even when I looked my prettiest there was always something else about me worth laughing at. Look, its Zelda (Tasrit)! The weird one. The awkward one who stutters. The one with a lazy eye (sometimes). The one with really dark circles! Look, it's the girl who is obsessed with weird things and she never talks about anything else other than languages and cultures! She acts like she is off her meds! People have always misunderstood me. They have always thought that I am weak. I was just trying to be happy. I was just trying to cope with my dark reality. Why did these people decide to do the same to me as all the others? Why did my suffering not cause that same kind of visceral effect I would feel if I witnessed someone in distress? If I witnessed *them* in distress? Am I some sort of superhuman then? Or are these people not human? They failed to realize that some of us are walking ticking bombs capable of detonating at any moment. We are not just *arbitrary stimuli*. I was not a fucking random Facebook profile that suddenly became a hologram that night with only one part of my body actually being real to his senses! It may be hollow *down there*, but I myself was not a hollow waste of space as I ended up becoming to him! We interact with the world and we are affected by the actions and words of others. They failed to realize that words have a lot of power, and so do the smallest actions. He thought I was a joking. He thought I was being dramatic. He failed to realize that to me he was not a piece of meat like I was to him. He was a human being that I wanted to explore more of and to love and respect. He failed to realize that he symbolized home for me. That *familiarity* and that *nostalgia* and that trust I had in him created a sensation *so powerful* it healed me from that very macabre experience that I had as a child. It healed me from the experience I had with my ex-husband too. To then experience the *striking contrast of it all*, contributed to this dreadful sensation of hopelessness and vulnerability. They have no idea how much I suffered all these months. I would wake up in the middle of night with cold sweats and heart palpitations. Intrusive thoughts of the argument would inundate my mind. His face, his voice, his presence would appear out of nowhere in my mind. I could not bear the notion of being ridiculed and used to that degree. It was and still is a major trigger or stressor. I would watch TV and I would start crying. I would begin to eat and I would start crying. I would try to sleep and I would start to cry hysterically. The idea of being anything less than human to him and a woman no longer desirable or never that desirable in the first place was incredibly intolerable. The mere idea of him being that much unkind to me was intolerable. I continue to have nightmares of this experience. The more I pretend he never existed, the more my body resents him. I may pretend to forget. I may pretend that everything is OK and that this never happened. But my body remembers and it will remember for some time. This is exactly the result of having PTSD and dealing with trauma. I must emphasize again they were both made aware of these conditions. I am sick and tired of people not understanding the implications of trauma and mental health issues. I hope they one day they reap what they sow. I hope they one day get to feel this same pain and dwell in it as much as I did because of them.

This man managed to completely break me. He was my catalyst. He shattered everything inside of me. He shattered my pride, my ego, my heart, my self worth, he shattered everything. He made me question myself, question everything. He shattered me and my perception of reality into a million pieces. He shattered my concept of humans, humanity, love, attraction, sexuality, sex, euphoria and dysphoria, happiness and sadness, rage and forgiveness, logic and absurdities. He shattered my self-image. He shattered my concept of good men and even bad men. He fragmented my concept of what is real and what is an illusion.

He fragmented my concept of Time. And yet...

He completely *transformed* me.

"To all of you who have shown no remorse
No compassion…
Your hypocrisy is my delirium
Your hypocrisy is my undoing

I am your sacrificial lamb?
You are all cruel fools!
May you all wail in pain as much as I have
I was the lamb blindfolded on your Eid
And you were the vicious slaughters
Vicious liars
What kind of humans are you to use someone's pain and
sheer agonizing confusion for your own twisted fairytale
ending?"

5. Mosaic

This man is so skilled in his gaslighting skills that he would make many people empathize with him with his "Let me respect you when you do, I will unblock you. I just have a lot of problems to deal with I don't have time for this (shit)." Till this day, I wonder if that was his way of showing he still cared about having me in his life. Of course, that is what I still would like to believe. He was never going to unblock me no matter what. Enough time passed by and he blocked me immediately when he saw my other account even though I was not "chasing him" deliberately. Still, I tried to apologize to him if he meant well and perhaps I failed to see that. There is a possibility he did manage to see or at least be aware of my messages. Nahara told me she confronted him about certain messages from my different accounts. Weren't they both made aware the ONLY thing I needed was him to tell me he doesn't hate me, and that he is sorry for hurting me? Then I remind myself that he was caught hiring prostitutes for his trip and that caused Nahara to pick a fight with him. At the same time, I had the genius idea to attempt to have a philosophical conversation about love and feelings with him the next day with my voice message. Best care scenario in the not so ruthless sense, I was seen as a little kid with an insignificant crush, and thus in his worldview that justified him blocking me. I was too young for him to take me emotionally and intellectually seriously all these years, but I was not too young to give him a very pleasurable night? I guess that isn't surprising for those actually well-versed in the world of men and sex huh? Fuck! In the worse care scenario, in the evil sociopathic sense, I was no longer useful to him and was perhaps given an ultimatum by Nahara. Block me or lose his wife. Or, block me or lose his luxurious trips to Aruba, Brazil, Germany, Portugal, and England. Which version reflects reality? Maybe it's a repulsive and disfigured mosaic of all of the above?

Dear Mr. Yaroud and Ms. Ruskin,

It incredibly pains me the journey you put me on. It incredibly pains me to realize you Brahim are completely oblivious to it all. I can't even say: "I should have never fallen in love with you, I should have never continued to message you, I should have never messaged Nahara—yet here *we* are." There is no we. I suffered alone while you continued to rejoice in your dark fake world. Here *I* am. Here I am yet again writing an imaginary letter. I fell in love and the reality is, I cannot unlove you entirely. I absolutely had no control over my emotions and there was no way I could have accepted the reality in front of me back then. My mind needed to rationalize what I was seeing and I needed to find justifications and logical explanations for your actions. There was absolutely no way to impede that thought process from happening. I am no longer blaming myself. True, I was wrong for having high expectations for someone like you. But that DOES NOT excuse you, and that will not stop me from getting the justice that I deserve. I will put you in your place one day. You will one day feel shame. You will never be happy being this much of a horrible person, and you will never find fulfillment nor success for doing this to me. Nahara, I believe you disappointed me the most, and I therefore don't have much words to say other than... Did we suffer together? Did we embark on a journey where we both felt each other's pain and then mocked each other's suffering? Or were you lost in your own ego this whole time? Are you both really that evil? You know Nahara, when I saw your photos. I really did not think you would have so much arrogance and bitterness inside of you. I specifically told myself I needed to let go of my love for Brahim for the sake of someone so innocent and pure like you. Did you not remember that from my audio message? "How can someone so dark be associated with someone so pure-hearted like you?" And this is how you repay me? You look the way you do and yet you acted and spoke to me as if you are an instagram 30-year old Kardashian bimbo who is entitled to have such an ego. Then people should treat you and talk down to you like an instagram 30-year old Kardashian bimbo. Learn your place as I have. Stay in your lane as I have. Be humble and act your part. Walk the walk and talk the talk that fits your character! It's that simple! Same goes for YOU...oh protagonist of my fucking story! You are not a 10. You were my 10. But inside and out you are a solid 5. Maybe 6. The women that you idealize and *actually desire the most* do not desire you back. So get off your fucking high horse because apparently the only "nurse" that you will find after riding it and getting hurt will be someone that looks like Nahara! Who apparently, TO YOU isn't enough if you constantly need to have sex with someone other than your own God damn wife. She is indeed beautiful and smart. She was just stupid to trust you. Nothing is enough for someone like you. And no one will ever be enough huh? You started to grow up more, learn more, work more, earn her trust and her wealth, you obtained more wealth somehow, then you began to work out more, and you noticed you could have someone better? You were 27 years old when you decided to marry someone with brains and beauty. More for her brains perhaps though? You think my above paragraphs were unhinged? Nope. You play with fire, expect to get burned! So, while yes

Nahara is beautiful, she just isn't your type Brahim now is she? I will be completely honest now that I have the liberty to do so, she is just not THAT sexy for you! I've seen your posts, and I have noticed your type too as much as you have noticed mine! Why then waste her time? Why use her like this. Why? Blonde American women for you POC, Mediterranean or North African men are meant for the stability, reputation and daily bread, but Mediterranean or women who remind you of Moroccan women are meant for the bed? You resent women from your country that much? You didn't want to deal with our passionate love and passionate dramatic bullshit, so you decided to get married with the complete opposite? Yet, you covet and desire that same passion from women who are or who are closer to your background. Interesting. I wonder also, how old were the *majority* of women you slept with? Hmmm…? Jesus Christ. Are you actually using Nahara only for her wealth Brahim are you? The cognitive dissonance is just TOO GOD DAMN painful! Besides socially awkward men like you have no business being assholes. You can't be both. Who wants to be in love with a socially awkward weird and creepy arrogant egotistical soulless JERK? I was told to stay in my lane all my life. I understand both of you wanted to "stand up" to me in your own ways during our own respective arguments. But you both absolutely had NO REASON to reveal your deadly fangs. How did you like mine? Sharp like shards of obsidian glass huh? Yet, I am truly exhausted. It's so nauseating to be gaslighted. Narcissism is so nauseating. The mere words themselves make me sick. I am so tired of using them. I am so tired of encountering them. I am really tired of encountering people who embody them. I am tired of unkind people. I am tired of this cycle of hate. But here "we" are…You can both kindly and respectfully go fuck yourselves. End Letter.

Oh Lord. That right there. That last letter. Holy Shit! That is the result of a cathartic catalytic effect! You insert a catalyst into a formula—BAM! Some shit is bound to happen and very quickly!! Inevitable. Imagine being THAT careless with what you post publicly on Facebook. Did it ever occur to them what someone in my position is capable of doing with that information? If they showed NO REMORSE for their words and actions, and if they showed ZERO self-control, restraint and fear, then neither will I! Reciprocity. Never underestimate the power of reciprocity.

I know what many of you may be thinking. "Daaamn JESUS CHRIST, Zelda? WTF?" You do understand that people have marital problems right? People cheat all the time and make mistakes all the time!" Nooooo really? Thank you so much for that enlightening and illuminating cliché behind our fallibility as homo fucking sapiens. Most people however….

EXPRESS REMORSE! Most people are capable of uttering "I'm sorry." Most people no matter the culture, faith or economic background, understand the implications behind hurting someone deeply when the person in question is highly sensitive, highly emotional and pure-hearted. And may I reiterate again….WHAT THE FUCK DID I HAVE TO DO WITH THEIR FUCKED UP MARITAL PROBLEMS? Go to a fucking therapist. Go to a strip club. Go have a threesome. Go fuck a fucking "Oh-La-La!" whore from a French brothel after having a Brazilian Brigadeiro smothered on a fucking English white fucking muffin in Aruba for fuck saaaakes if you were THAT bored of your "wife" or if you were THAT pissed of at her. YOU DO NOT have sex with someone who has posted for YEARS about men gaslighting her and about narcissism specifically! I have posted for YEARS the same content over and over about North African men taking advantage of me and causing me a lot of harm. He fucking knew about my past experiences. HE KNEW!! Why did he have to be just like the rest or even worse? I had "she is an awkward neurodivergent nerdy young lady who is incredibly fragile, innocent and totally capable of falling in love quickly" written all over my fucking face. Why then treat me like I was the Instagram/TikTok evil bimbo? You know what Brahim could have done to yield a much more healthier and positive outcome? He could have taken advantage of me AND THEN thrown the "I am married" bomb at my fucking face at the hotel room. If he just wanted sapiosexual sex from a cute, exotic yet weird Facebook famous Mediterranean/Native American/North African Jewish, Turkish/Persian at the time 31-year old "Lolita" before his Moroccan balls get older like a pile of *barqoq*… why then not just tell me the truth after "finishing?" Why would he care if I hypothetically threw a fit over it? (I would have not been able to process that AT ALL anyway so 99% sure I would have shrugged it off!) He could have left the room satisfied, and then blocked me on Facebook. I would have been a little upset maybe even deeply disappointed to where I'd make a simple post or video about it, but I would have laughed it off and get over it in a couple of days. That would have at least saved me the pain of falling deeply in love with him. It would have kept me from messaging him and thinking about him so much. I would have never noticed him looking at my pictures again. I would have never asked him if he wanted to hook up again. None of that would have happened had he just been transparent with me from that night at the Robert Treat Hotel. To be completely honest with you, he could have told me he

95

was married from the very beginning and perhaps…I would have not cared and slept with him. I would have not known who Nahara is. I wouldn't know how she looked like.

I wouldn't have formed an idea of her being a benign person. I would have not imagined her in pain. Don't judge me here. This is also a problem with struggling with PTSD. You live moments as if they are dreams sometimes. I was still processing my encounter with my Afghan dating app companion, and I was therefore honestly having a hard time processing Brahim/Yugerthen in front of me. I have never been with two different men in a such a short amount of time. Sensations of confusion and guilt stemming from my religious background also had a lot to do with it. But if I knew from that night that he was a married man or a man in some sort of a romantic serious relationship I swear on the life of all the cats in Istanbul I WOULD HAVE NEVER ALLOWED MYSELF TO FALL IN LOVE WITH HIM! None of that would have happened if he were just honest with me. He could have still gotten what he wanted. Win/Win situation. It would have been incredibly unethical of both of us, but at least I would have felt enough remorse to be the one to block him or leave him alone. It is incredibly perplexing as to why he didn't weigh the pros and cons of his actions that night and thereafter if he feared either losing his wife or his life of luxuries. In the end, Nahara wasn't worth someone defending anyway. I am not so sure what mirror I broke or what witch did I piss off prior to this event? What saint, holy alter, or talisman did I desecrate? What god did I piss off? Or did I upset The God/Hashem/Allah? I said my prayers. I repented of my own sins. My suffering will end soon. There are consequences to actions. One should never undermine or underestimate the power of a domino effect. The most important realization from this entire experience is something that I had mentioned earlier: Nahara was my second and main catalyst for writing this book. She made me believe Brahim denied cheating on her with me and convinced her to mock me out of revenge. That's how it seemed to me. Even if he is some sort of unapologetic passenger in this whole journey, that too is just incredibly malevolently surreal. I need to restate this quote from Nahara: "Maybe stop meeting up with strange men and you will finally stop putting yourself in harms way!" Let this be CLEAR: She is admitting "her man" is dangerous and caused me harm. What a disturbing woman. You know the Bible says "love is not boastful." But I guess Brahim decided to take that to A WHOLE NEW LEVEL by deciding to keep quiet all these years about "his love" for her. He did not even bother to defend her when I posted a bunch of comments on her account. Strange. Bottom line is I was targeted. Targeted like prey. I feel deeply disgusted! Yet I am tempted to say…. I wrote this so that he could one day read this and apologize to me. But I know that will never happen. Yes, I know I am very contradictory. That's kinda one of the many themes of this damn (but very precious) book. Do I want them to feel shame? Do I want to hurt them both? Do I want revenge or do I want a happy ending? That ship has honestly sailed. We have reached the point of no return. That is the point. I secretly want to forgive them both, but the sensation of humiliation is far too great. If this man truly has an antisocial personality disorder, then there is no way he would be able to process any of this. But I therefore do need to teach him a lesson. "I listened to your voice messages again, and I realized you were trying to hurt me with mentioning the age gap with Brahim!" Nahara stated that day. I swear on my life if you were to listen to my audios it would be clear as a dress on Bianca Censori that my intentions were BENIGN!! Innocent!!

97

From the moment I start talking till the very end, your heart will break when you hear the duress in my voice. I sound like a little kid. I sound very humble and grounded in the facts. Ugh. I sound like your textbook trauma victim. I was essentially experiencing something called "regression" in psychology. But she acted like your textbook trauma victim too. Perhaps she was experiencing regression too. Perhaps Brahim as well? Maybe he had a horrible childhood and something snapped in his brain to make him want to behave in destructive ways? I have gone over this already. I sincerely still don't know who was behind that idea of posting that photo. I sincerely still don't know if Brahim/Yugerthen truly denied everything and was the one to brainwash her to believe that I was a liar. Who is the culprit? The fact is they are both guilty. They had the choice to do right by me, they chose otherwise. It's simple. For two grown ass adults to do this kind of a number on someone innocent is extremely heart-breaking. Imagine actually getting to the point where I profoundly felt "love in humanity" for Brahim. He is not even worth something so pure as that.

What's that saying again? "It's the quiet ones you need to look out for!" Definitely true. People need to learn: Words have the power to destroy and the power to heal. Words are attached to intention and states of mind. His actions and words occurred under a state of mind of egotistical panic and rage. Her words and actions occurred under a state of mind of not only egotistical panic and rage, but of a sort of defeatist envy as well. All of my words and actions towards them occurred under a defeatist state of mind of rage and sorrow. There is a *huge* difference. "Yes I have seen your messages, that was one of the many things I found on the most recent time that I

98

confronted him," Nahara said to me that day. A little bit of what I wrote in my "imaginary letters" were actually a combination of things I last sent him on Messenger. Meaning, I did give a context or background about myself that I naively thought would help him change his mind. I mentioned the abuse I endured as a kid, I mentioned how I have always felt like the freak of nature among my peers, and I mentioned how everything combined and with what happened between us led me to have thoughts of ending my own life. I explained how that contributed to me feeling unworthy as a person and ostracized by Brahim, and thus causing me terrible PTSD flare ups. I mentioned in the messages that I had ASD, and I gave reasonable justifications for the way I spoke during our argument in January. Yes. I took it that far! I needed him to know that I wasn't acting as a child due to being some sort of spoiled brat as he thought, I was essentially regressing due to that classic flight or fight response. Yes. I was THAT technical with him. How neurodivergent of me... I mentioned that the most important thing that I needed from Brahim was simply closure or <u>ending things on good terms</u>. She saw that, she then realized those messages came from me when I told her, and she ultimately decided to treat me ruthlessly just like Brahim. I may not have the complete puzzle figured out of those despotic individuals, but I hope you now have the fragments of my puzzle completed now. This is the reason why I am more enraged with Nahara than I am with Brahim. I expected more out of her. There is nothing more evil than a woman who consciously decided to degrade another woman without any remorse. If she knew Brahim and I were exchanging messages, why did she allow for our interactions to get this far? So many questions. So many speculations. So many *dark conclusions* I do not actually want to believe, but they may very well be the only reality.

I know I sounded very angry and hateful throughout many sections of this book, but I am not going to be a hypocrite and apologize for that. I don't think I have to state this, but for what is worth it should be clear once more that I was using a very particular alter ego there, not just in my "letters." That being said that "push and pull" sensation between resignation and retribution still lingers. Why do people put us in that kind of a position in the first place where we feel that kind of hatred? It is very painful. Do you know how many times I have been told I love to "play the victim," and I love to act like such a "martyr?" FYI: I have edited the shit out of many sections of this book. Particularly how I expressed myself over Frenchtown's beloved holistic vet. I didn't actually wanted to call her a buck teeth bitch. I have the power to edit that out whenever I want to. But the only reason why I decided to leave that section as it is was to prove a point. Stating the obvious in case some people just did not understand the assignment. I wish Nahara could have edited her words to me that day. You know Facebook/WhatsApp/Instagram now has a bit of a longer "grace period" to edit the messages you send. I wish she could have taken advantage of that. If only people would edit spoken words. If only people could edit thoughts before pressing "send" as easily as editing a book. So please. Do not judge me. You add lithium to a container of water, you will get a reaction. It is SIMPLE. If in nature you have chemicals that are highly reactive more than others, how could we ignore that notion among ourselves as human beings? I was a balloon filled with hydrogen gas minding my own business, then along came Brahim and added in his horny oxygen into my space, and Nahara then ignited me with her envious spiteful fire. BOOM! What do people expect? These elements are what they are intrinsically, and there is nothing that we can do to stop a reaction when it begins (I am trying my best at using scientific analogies, sorry towards the chemistry community for any discrepancies!) But these are inanimate substances that have no ethics, no concept of morality nor decision making skills. We as humans we are who we are intrinsically, but our environment can also shape us. It is in our nature to have the ability to stop and think before we act to avoid feeling pain or causing pain. We have the ability to say sorry when we do cause that pain intentionally or unintentionally. My pain was like styrofoam dissolved in acetone by them both—it was easily done away with. (Yes, I am a huge fan of NileRed on Youtube.) But please, these analogies aren't meant to be just a desperate attempt at me being witty. They are sincerely meant for you to reflect. There is nothing more that I desire than forgiveness. I was desiring that for months. In all honesty, I feel that I still love Yugerthen/Brahim whenever I feel an overwhelming sensation of hatred towards him, and conversely I feel like I completely loathe him whenever I feel an overbearing sensation of mercy for him. I desperately did not want to hate Brahim nor Nahara, but they left me no choice. People have no idea how much I kept imagine him finally reaching out to me and apologizing. I imagined him in tears. I imagined him human. I imagined her crying asking me for forgiveness too. But it seems I was deemed unworthy of humanity. The part of my brain that stems from trauma has gone as far as imagining him doing the complete opposite. I had this intense fear that he would totally lose it with my messages that he would tell me to go kill myself. And I had fears that the tension between me and Nahara would end up in: "And on the next episode of Dateline…" Yeah. My mind actually went there. Tragic isn't it? He honestly does not deserve any of it however! Neither forgiveness nor resentment. Neither love nor hatred. He deserves to be forgotten. But it is what it is… isn't it? I need therefore to finish processing my pain. I want the world to know there are those of us who have been wronged way too many times and we want the satisfaction of "revenge." Let me have it. Let me be human. I want to put them in their places *like humans do.*

Butterfly effect, domino effect, catalytic chaos…

CRACK! SNAP! BAM! BOOM! All over the floor….

A mosaic of reality, truth and clarity married with illusions, falsehood and obscurity…

"Did you imagine this would happen?" Brahim said as he finished kissing me. He was asking me if I knew we would meet to then make love. How romantic I thought! I said: "Yeah, I guess!" "You guessed? Good!" That "good" ladies and gentlemen will forever echo in my mind. The way he uttered that word and in the manner in which he did, sends chills down my spine. Did he ever imagine the consequences of that one night? Did I? Had he only reacted in the way I presented in my parallel universes earlier these profound emotions would have eventually faded away. It would have never reached the surface, and they would have never been unearthed in the manner in which it happened. Let's say this altogether I-R-O-N-Y! What does that fucking spell? Irony. He took that original voice message too seriously. I sounded very poetic, well because that is how I talk and how I experience emotions. I had approached him in resignation. I knew he wouldn't reciprocate my "love" and he didn't have to. We could have still seen each other hypothetically. I understand that the universe obviously did not want that for me. But I am human, a woman, and I can not help but think this way. It wasn't until after the fact, after the unraveling of said events, that this profound "love" was manifested so overtly and powerfully. I realized how much I actually did love him when I started to realize the impact his actions made. I still wonder: Why cheat so openly? Why take that risk in the first place? Did Nahara know about me from the very beginning? Did she hear my original voice message to Brahim? Did she change her status to "It's Complicated" because of me? Did she see the messages between us this whole time? Did Brahim keep blocking me because he could actually have feelings for me? Could he potentially fall in love with me? Does it really matter? It would be one heck of a plot twist. But it wouldn't absolve him. It would only make him even more of a coward. If Nahara really wanted to make me scream in envy, why not post a photo where Brahim is kissing her on the cheek or kissing her *passionately*? Are these two actually in a relationship or is there a major context that I have been missing? All these questions and more continue to echo in my mind till this day.

 Oh so called protagonist of my story, if I could only have you in front of me right now, I would want to tell you: "You were a beautiful man to me too as you are to Nahara. I saw the beauty in your darkness. I saw the beauty in your awkwardness. I saw you for you. I really did. I still wish to understand the root of your hostility towards me. *Makh leeghee tijraHt zund gheeka?* Why did you hurt me this way? Who was I to you all these years? The community that you know, I know. Your friends are my friends. You have known me for years. Why was I your target? Why was I your prey? Why was I your little plaything? I am indeed someone who was taken seriously by many people who needed an advocate for their basic human rights in your country. They tell me they love me as their sister. I see them as my family. Did you not understand the philosophical implications of me being a part of your world? I speak your language as if it were my own, and at some point in time it was part of my own lineage. Ergo, I saw YOU as my own brother. I saw you as part of my family way before you mentioned that I could meet you years ago. That line of thinking is not delusional. Brotherhood and sisterhood are very strong cultural concepts among North Africans and in predominant Muslim societies in general. Everyone calls each other *Uma/Gma* (brother) or *Ultma* (sister) in your language. God is my witness, I truly thought of you as someone sensitive. I thought of you as someone worthy of knowing and understanding. With enough time and after meeting you, I then thought of you as someone worthy of loving and forgiving. I would have forgiven you had you told me the truth that night or even that day we had our argument. I needed to have closure with someone I felt was a part of my family all these years. Why couldn't you face me? Did it ever occur to you that we could cross paths one day? What would you say to me? What are you going to say to me now? Was my involvement in your community a joke as I was to you? It's one thing to be considered so childish and immature and naive as a woman, it's another thing entirely different to be considered all of that as a person who's passion, commitment, and knowledge revolved around your people who are themselves constantly undermined. Will you ever understand the cognitive dissonance and the philosophical irony behind any of this Yugerthen? For someone who pays attention to freedom and justice in a governmental system, you sure know how to make a female feel incredibly oppressed and invalidated from her psyche to her core. Did I actually become completely obsolete to you? You sincerely do not care whether I live or die? Do have have any idea how much your words and that photo made me wish I were dead? Irony of ironies..this all happened because I wanted to give you words full of genuineness and life. Would you then still have the cynical audacity to confront me over the contents of this book? Who the fuck were you to trick me the way you did, to charm your way into my deep labyrinth they way you did, and treat me like a mediocre childish whore? I lost my dignity on October 16, 2023 ending up madly infatuated with a devious devilish man involved in a complicated relationship. It's so wrong, and yet it's not my fault. You lost your humanity a long time ago. On January 28, 2024, I lost mine. For your precious FYI: If you were to ever offer me the explanation that I longed for, and the apology that I deserve, I too would offer you my apologies for the content written in this book. But you ultimately deserved it all. I hope one day I will be able to forgive you. It was a pleasure (or not?) meeting you after all, Goodbye…

Well…I obviously chose the wrong Moroccan man AGAIN. Although I obviously need to stop romanticizing bad people, I will not fall for the trap of generalizing either! Not all Moroccan or North African men are the same. Not all men are the same period! I am *mature* enough to know this! My dear friends from Agadir, Morocco are all aware of this story. "We do not claim him" my friend Anir stated proudly in a comment. Thank you! I would love to say to them that they are the true gems of my world. I love you all with all of my heart and soul. You all have supported me throughout this journey. I know many of you actually took my passion for Amazigh culture and language seriously. Many of you indeed never undermined my efforts to help those needing basic human rights in your country. A special shoutout to all those friends. May you get everything your hearts desire!

Could I forgive Nahara too one day? I swear to God I would if she realized she made a horrible mistake. I never wanted to have these thoughts. But: "I feel like I'm in a dreamlike state.. in a haze.. I can't process this.." I told her in my audio messages. Does that sound like someone deliberately wanting to "break up" her marriage? No. Not at all!!

Reciprocity…never underestimate the value of reciprocity!

6.Poetic Justice

I started writing my first poems of passion while being madly in love with him around January of last year 2024. They were ultimately modified after the unraveling of specific events of course. Other poems clearly manifest my rage and sorrow as I explained earlier. "*The actions we do, no matter how minimal send a message.*" All these months I have been feeling like my life has been hanging on by a thread. People have no idea that from the very first grapheme of this book till the very end, I have been experiencing painful intrusive thoughts of the whole journey. I am still struggling with my self-image and self-worth till this day because of him. I still imagine myself dead so that this pain could end. Inner-strength. I am trying to hang on to my inner-strength as much as I can. If only people practiced reciprocity. If only people practiced transparency. If only people could be reminded of humanity this world would be a little more healthier. I wish I could wish them well, but the best I can do is ask God or the universe to grant them what they deserve. I curse the day I landed in Newark. And other times, I reminisce of that night over and over and over again. I close my eyes and I can see every fiber, every shade of color and every shape or pattern of that night with him. I remember when he specifically showed me the New York skyline from the window as he tried to get closer to me from the side. He was trying to be romantic. How sweetly devious of him. From the moment I waited for him at the airport, till the moment he last texted me the day after, the events in Elizabeth/Newark replay in my mind so softly and majestically. It then follows by sharp flashbacks of what ended up unfolding afterwards. It feels like violent ocean waves purposely drowning the shit out of you. Using a different analogy as a way to stay true to the theme of this book, I should rather say it feels like shards of glass detonating in your face! Ergo the sensation is quite unpleasant and very unsettlingly indeed. I have to find a way to cope with that. By writing. Creating. Producing. Manifesting. I took chaos and turned into beauty. That is profound.

Below you will find my works of *unorganized literary thoughts* that I courageously call "poems." Obviously, what I **now** feel as "love" or "love in humanity" or even "hatred" has completely changed in the span of about one year. Some of my writings should make you smile, laugh hysterically, or cry uncontrollably. Heck some of the things I wrote are pretty stupid and some things are truly just *art for art sake*. But those ideas are honestly the most enjoyable. But as a reminder, what I endured was not funny. Humiliation is a powerful sensation. Unrequited love, desire, respect and kindness are all powerful concepts. So is *poetic justice.*

Thank you for entering the first door into my labyrinth of events and getting this far. Now welcome inside my gouged perforated unorganized poetic world. Welcome inside my mind of *lost passions* and *fragmented nostalgia...* Welcome inside the labyrinth of my mind of *fragmented love and shattered hopes* from a very much *fragmented and broken perception of reality.*

-Bride of the Rain

1. Flashback

Your eyes are tattooed against mine

I can't unsee you

The fragrance of your eyes

I sigh

I cry

The unsettling image of your grin

The atmosphere of your presence

Still torments my memory

Still lingers in my mind

But I remain invisible…

Anonymous

A mistake

Insignificant to you

It's not fair it's not fair

Why must I suffer in this affair

Your image

I wish it was gone

The more I realize you hate me

The more I want you gone

Your image

Your eyes

The regard of someone so cruel

So lost

And yet I found you

I found myself deep inside that gaze

I hate this pain

I loathe this game

The ones you love never love you back

The ones you love betray you the most

The ones that take away your breath suffocate you the most

I hate this pain

I hate love

I hate your eyes flashing before mine

I hate you

I hate you so much

I hate that I still love you

I hate that I can't find any logic in this

I hate the fact that even though you chose to completely forget about me,

I can never forget you.

I can never forget the beauty in loving you

End.

2. Rainbow

Emerald eyes
That I despise*
I envy her
She has your attention
And I have your aversion
How is that fair oh wise protagonist of my story?
If you were to die a million deaths she would only
"Sad" react to the news, while I would cry for all eternity.
She would be too pretentious to even look at you the same
way I do. You desire that which is forbidden. Unattainable.
Her heart does not flutter when she thinks of you like mine.
Her insides do not turn when she hears your name like mine.
Frivolous interactions. Aren't we all? In your ostentatious
matrix. Meaningless yet some are worthy in your sphere than
others. It does not seem to bother you, oh wise protagonist
of my story. To know that she would never give you the same
attention as you do to her. She wouldn't give you her time like
I would. She wouldn't even give you one night. And yet I am
the one who is ostracized? Don't give me your wrath now.. it
is not because you are not worth it. No! But a woman like her
is a Queen from a different dimension!
Emerald eyes.. pale skin of silk…Sunkissed hair. Women like
her are your ultimate objects of desire? Impossible. For her
not to know which Bride of the Rain you had in your grasp
one night and which one dominates your mind. Lies, lies…
Everything must be a lie!!! Three brides and only one groom.
Who will you choose? Oh oops. So one pseudo wife and two
brides who will you choose? Yes I know who. Why torment
my mind like this? If that Bride of the Rain was your Queen
then I was your dark sorceress that night. I don't have

113

emerald eyes. I don't have pale skin of silk. I don't have sunkissed hair. But I had you in my grasp. I enjoyed you at least for a while. You may have that bitter memory or you may have forgotten. I have that sweet memory and it will never be forsaken. But it does beg the question. Why did you choose this Bride of the Rain last year to irrigate your drought? There must of have been something about me that you needed to experience? What may that be?

Emerald eyes I don't have, but I had eyes of Semitic majesty. Pale Skin of silk I don't have but I have rough skin of Silk Road honey, maize and olives. Sunkissed hair I don't have but I have hair of Saharan blues and Persian setars. My mind is a labyrinth of wild passion. Her mind is a straight path of emptiness. She possesses all that which you admire. Beauty and intelligence? And yet am supposed to believe you made your way into my labyrinth just to reach the southern entrance? Well then I guess I should feel flattered. I got to experience all facets of you. Your smile, your frown, your joy, your anger, your energy, your exhaustion, your urge that night , your avoidance , your attention, your indifference, your shyness, your ruthlessness, your awkwardness, your assertiveness, your everything. I feel honored oh protagonist of my story. That I was at least the Bride of the Rain and the withered flower to experience loving you ardently.

End.

3. Prince of the South

Prince of the south

Mysterious warlock

You were quietly around

You crept into my life

Like a snake across a river

You had this persona , this aura , this energy about you

That I could not ignore nor forsake

You had me fooled

Just like someone in power and with powers would

I remember you from before

That star you skip while counting the night sky

Prince of the south

Conquerer of hearts

Conquerer of all

You appeared out of nowhere in my life
Snatching my soul

Captivating me with your sinister smile

Your sword of arrogance pierced me in pieces

You had a mission

And you succeeded.

Mysterious warlock…

Oh brahmin*

Of a mighty caste…

Bring me your tea and spices

And I will fulfill any task

Like the infinite spirals of a million grape vines

That's how my love and my wrath give birth to these lines

But go on…

Pretend like I don't exist

Like I don't matter

And I will move on

Oh Mr. "Go away"

Monsieur, "Leave me alone"

Oh brahmin of a mighty caste…

You had me under a spell

An evil power…

All under a mask

Take your scent with you

It is no longer pleasant to keep.

To your arrogant world of meaningless colors

A tapestry of hate…

I exalted you on a throne

But like a conniving sultan

You exiled me so you can be left alone.

You won

I lost.

You have conquered my heart and my mind

Only to destroy them piece by piece

Slowly all within time.

Oh brahmin

Of a mighty caste.

Your are an army of one

A ruthless soldier who kills to steal the crown

But please don't frown

Your reputation is surely your pride

My eyes, my skin, my voice

My life…

Was to You nothing but a joy ride.

Go on then…
To your world of duty without beauty

To your web of mysteries and countless lies

Oh brahmin..

Of a mighty caste

You insolent fool

Your kingdom will fall

Your reign is only temporary

The knight of nights

The dice of Days

Time is ticking

And karma awaits

Go then,

Far far away from me.

Your toxic touch burns inside of me

I don't want the memory of your hands on me

I don't want the memory of your lips on mine

I don't want the memory of you inside

I don't want the memory of your eyes over mine

I don't want the false memory of you being kind.

How did I ever encounter

Such a being like you.

What mirror did I break

For this agony to become my fate ?

To love someone so irate

To love someone with so much hate

To love someone with an ego so great?

To love someone so dark and twisted.

To love someone so calculating and clever

And yet so ungrateful , unpleasant and unwise…

Oh brahmin…
Of such a mighty caste

Take me please
I beg you take me
To the past.

Where our paths did not cross

How did we get to this point?
I am at a loss ….

Oh brahmin of a mighty caste

How does it feel to get everything done , everything you want
And anyone you want?

At the expense of someone's pain and sanity!?

Go then!!!!

Off you go

Into the desert of illusions
To a mountain of confusion

Oh brahmin

Of a superior caste …

Enjoy of whatever wasted wealth and youth you may have

One day you will also become just dust

Like the kind I became for you the day you couldn't even say goodbye.

You enticed me with the most dangerous of spells

Set me free please I kindly request

That you release me from your grasp

I do not want to harm you

So I do not want to be harmed

Despite the damage already being done…

You can give me my peace now
I am no longer your burden your problem.

Prince of the south
With skin of golden cinnamon
And eyes as dark as henna

Your heart can't be that cold
Your heart can't possibly be that broken

You can't possibly be that cruel

Prince of the south
With skin of golden cinnamon
And eyes as dark as henna

Your breath was as warm as mint tea
On a cold desert night

And your touch was so sublime...

The euphoria of it all ...
Was exquisitely divine

Oh Prince of the south

Mysterious warlock

Conquerer of hearts

Conquerer of all

*the brahmin caste system in India is considered to be the most prestigious of
all comprised of mainly high priests.

4. Your Shadow

You left a deep scar in my memory
Unforgettable
So unforgettable there's no room for regret
So painful there's not even room for rage

I know, if you were to see these lines
Your heart will laugh, your dark soul will only feel more
empowered

How I wish something could come over you..

So that you could maybe be possessed with the smallest
amount of remorse as possible

Just a little bit of shame
Just a little bit of pain
Just a little bit of regret
Of how you treated me.

I know I am insane (to you)
But at least I rejoice in my insanity

I sadly can't say the same for you
While you suffer in silence in your vanity

I think..
Maybe..
Just maybe..

I was never in love with you

But with a memory

Only a distinct version of you

The negative

The opposite

The upside down

I am severely shocked

I have lost, you have won

I am weak you are strong

How does it feel to have this victory ?

Your shadow tricked me into thinking I was in love with you…
Your shadow was the one who enticed me.
Your shadow is to blame.

The dark side of you caressed me that night
And all I wanted to do was to be your healer
Your guide. A source of happiness and relief.
I fell in love with your shadow. And it is your shadow that
wanted me…
I fell in love with your shadow. And it is that dark entity that
was kind to me.

5. The Storm

Irony of ironies

Allegories and myths

A legend of deep love
Lost inside a mist

It rains..

It pours..

Thunder plays in the background

To the best beat humanity can witness

The chant of victory

A cry of War

A call of Revenge

ROAR! Roaring across the skies.

These waters come marching down

One drop of wisdom

The other of shame

One drop of excitement

The other of pain

Contradictions, opposites

It is quite strange to find beauty in something so fearful and dangerous.

That is how I feel towards my love for you.

It has no logic
Other than the symbols and meanings we humans give to other humans.

I have completely lost my mind.

While I dance under this storm.

I wave a white flag of surrender!

Yet lightening strikes at the top!

Hilarious.

I tried to play nice and yet I almost died.

Enjoying something many of us would think is joyful

Contemplating something so natural.

I lost my mind.

I have gone completely mad.

Over you and only you.

A woman with a tragic end

Emotions with a majestic middle

Two friends with an ordinary beginning

How I wish I could wash away those memories

In midst of this storm.

Perhaps… in another lifetime in some distant past… We could have had a love story worthy of praise, worthy of tributes and accolades

Talks of the imaginary, talks of shadows…
Of hypotheticals and "what ifs"

Legends among legends

Esoteric ideas among mystics doctrines

Fiction along with imagination….

You were the one. You were the one to break me.

You were the one to inspire me. The one to revive the artist in me, the dreamer in me, the healer in me.

You were it. You were my storm to transform my life. To transform it all……

6. Bride of the Rain (Your Shadow Pt. 2) (me...)

I offer you these lines, a symbol of my forgiveness
Lines of purity

You left a deep scar in my memory.
So unforgettable there's no room for regret
So painful there's no room for rage.

Everyone tells me to forget
Everyone tells me to move on

But no one understands that I feel the spectrum of colors that
make me happy and sick and that I can taste and smell the
emotions behind inferno red or paradise blue

No one understands
The scent of humiliation still lingers
The touch of regret still echoes
The taste of disbelief still whispers
Inside of me.

And the thought of revenge
Flirts with my mind.

That has entertained me for a while
The thought has been in the air
It goes away, then returns in its finest form

And when the day comes when I act upon this anger, I would
just tell you that I was not going to...
but hey I changed me mind like humans do....

I wanted to be your source of light.
And that's the path that I will choose
(Or not?…)

I wanted to be some sort of healer
To get rid of all your wounds
(Or not?…)

There was so much mystery in your eyes
Yet too much darkness
There was so much kindness and innocence in those eyes
Yet now all I see is something rotten and decayed

How does it feel to win this victory ?
You two may call me crazy
But at least I rejoice in my insanity
While you all suffer in silence in your vanity!

When I think about how you treated me,
And how you continue to laugh while I cry
And how you continue to live life as if I never existed.
All my insides go numb by the hour
How does it feel to have everything your heart desires?
How does it feel to have that much power?

It's in those moments when the spirit of revenge comes back
to torment me like a storm drowns a blooming flower.

I am the original Bride of the Rain…
And she has cried many showers…

7. Deja Vu

You made yourself an abode inside my memories.

But…

I promise you I'm trying my best to forget you!

To forget those kind eyes

I wanted so badly for this to be the last poem about you.

But I couldn't keep that promise. I am sorry.

I at least promise you that you will disappear from my mind after.

I promise …I will try!

Part of me wants to hold on to that special memory.

That night I had you in my arms.

That night I felt like I could spend eternity embracing you. Past present and future combined.

Time became significant and simultaneously meaningless…

You became someone from my childhood, an embodiment of innocence, a spec of deja vu … a past memory from another life…a fulfillment of my Gilgul*.

You became a glimpse of what could become. Of a hypothetical love.
Passionate. Pure. Genuine. Trust.

I loved you I really did

I deeply loved you with so much strength

But I have to find a way to let go.

I will try my best.

I promise, to finally let you go!

When I think about how little I matter to you

It's easier to find that path ….

That leads you into total oblivion
In the in between.
In an abyss…
In a limbo…
Nowhere. But somewhere in the forgotten.

No… no…I can't…
I refuse to forget and let these memories crumble.

But when I remember how much you hurt me

It makes it easier to let you go.

But before you go…

I just wish you could say sorry.

You took me on this agonizing train ride with no beginning and no end.

Why can't you apologize?

Get out!!!

I don't want you anymore.

Get out of my mind.

Get out of my soul.

Get out of my heart.

You don't deserve me.

Get out of my poems.

Get out of my songs.

Get out of my spirit.

Get out of my thoughts.

Go away!
And leave me alone!!!!!

This melody is ready to come to an end

This novel is ready to wrap up...

This ride is ready to be over.

I am ready to stop writing.
I am ready to become silent.

I want there to be emptiness again...

Because when I am reminded of you...

My world is filled with the sounds and images of what could
have been and of what should have been

Instead I want to focus on what there is and where I am
now....

A paint brush of reality
With strokes of truth

The colors of unrequited love.

A crimson red of hatred
A stormy grey of dissension...

The painting is finished.

I have the full picture. And then suddenly...

This story feels unfinished
This journey feels not over
This experience feels incomplete

I am in complete shock
When I realize how much of an impact you made on my life

For you to faze me like this
It's unforgivable
Unimaginable...

Unbelievable how your presence is still here
How did you manage to have that much power over me
Over my heart.

You are still here.
Still inside my head...
Still Inside my mind.
You made yourself an abode inside my memories...

And then suddenly...
when I imagine you gone...
books forget their titles
Poems forget their stanzas
Songs forget their choruses
These pages disappear
These lines diminish
These words fall asleep
These emotions that began it all...
Fade away slowly...
To the beginning where there was no reason to write a stupid
book of poems
No reason at all.
End Cycle...Repeat.

*Gilgul is the esoteric Jewish concept of reincarnation. The belief that
souls "migrate" (transmigration of souls) to another body after death. It
is the idea that a specific task must be fulfilled in order to achieve peace
and happiness.*

8. Master of disguise

Master of Disguise, Master of manipulation …

You sure had me fooled.

I never thought you would be the one

Out of all the men I've met in my life so far,

I never thought you'd be the one to deceive me the most.

I never thought you would make me cry

I actually never thought the idea itself would make you think….

That I am childish.

Immature you say?

To feel pain? To be angry ? To be so disappointed in someone you feel that your mind and your body are no longer one.

An out of body experience they call it.

Indeed I experience that a lot.

I couldn't recognize myself that day. And I couldn't recognize you. I couldn't recognize what was in front of me. Nothing made sense.

Nothing seemed real. Nothing mattered.

In that moment all I wanted to do is close my eyes and disappear. Perhaps close my eyes and have you in front of me instantly. Perhaps close my eyes and have nothingness consume me and abandon this pain. I wanted to abandon this earth.

I desperately wanted to still believe

That you were good.

That you were different.

That you were the person that lived inside my imagination.

I never felt so humiliated in my life.

I remember I said that to you.

Do you remember?

What demon possessed you? What dybbuk torments you? What jinn is in love with you? For you to behave like you have no soul?

Was I that easy of a sacrifice?

"Night with my man" huh?

Carrie's bloody fucking prom night rather...

How fucking dare you.

Master of disguise

Master of manipulation

The face of Hypocrisy. Lunacy. Chaos.

Bravo! I could learn a trick or two from the likes of you.

End.

9. Amanita Muscaria

You are not just my forbidden fruit
You are my toxic mushroom
With one bite you die
And yet I've never felt so alive

For days and days I've felt dead inside
But with just one bite
I can now see the world and its lies

Where were you all these years ?
You are a blessing in disguise
I cursed the day I met you
I cursed the day I took that bite
But I will never regret loving you

It was your poison that opened my eyes
To the reality of life
To the darkness that dwells inside
And yet you are my light

I see things so clearly now
Specs of red and white
Swirls of orange and green

I hallucinate you all day
I am high on this love

But whether my soul leaves this earth
Or I survive this ride ....

You will eventually fade away
Quietly
Silently
In the background
This love will lose its sound

No noise
No images

Only remnants decaying
Slowly
Gently
In the background

My toxic mushroom
My reality
Amanita muscaria…

10. I (still) love him

I still love him.. (well..)
I could yell it at the whole world
That you are mine
He is mine
Not yours!

The end?

The end…

THE END!!!

But there's no end when there's unfinished business
Incomplete robotic sentences
Undotted Turkish ı's

What Moorish prayer do I have to make
In order to end these thoughts of him
What Semitic lamb do I have to sacrifice ?
What Ottoman talisman should I wear?
What African spell should I chant?
For the universe to help me get rid of him from my mind and
soul?
I want this end.
This needs to end.
All songs and stories come to an end
What comes up eventually comes down
What has life eventually expires
I loved him
I still do…. (Not exactly..)
I want to yell it to the whole world…

That I am so messed up
Broken
Fucked up
For loving someone who's mind is fixated on someone else…
For loving someone who's mind is fixated on… *things* in thongs….
Finally, this has an end.

11. I Lost It

I loved you like a deranged person
That's loved in past tense
But I'm still deranged

That hasn't changed

How is it that I am fuming with so much anger and drowning in pain and disbelief
And still admit that I once loved you.

With the type of love that makes you want to sing

Write

Compose

Create

Rejoice

Lust

Dream

Dance

Smile

Delight

Melodramatic, romantic, cheesy, passionate, pure , innocent and genuine

But utterly stupid.

I was stupidly in love.

I was stupid.

To think you would possibly feel just a little bit… just a little… of appreciation for me.
Even just a little bit of love.
End.

12. Luckiest Man Alive

Luckiest man alive
For someone so godless
He is sure looking out for you...
You are invincible. Unfazed by everything.
You are so powerful. Not even a hex could affect you.
You have everyone fooled.
Except for me.
Luckiest man alive...
One day that smirk on your face will be replaced with slime.
So godless yet God chose you over me. You got away with
everything and you have your way with everyone. Why?
Elohai, Elohai, lama samachtani?
Why have you abandoned me oh Lord?
Why show him mercy? Am I supposed to love him as my
enemy? Or am I supposed to hate him as my ex-friend
Luckiest man alive. For someone so godless, He has
preferred you.

13. One Off Situation

I'm not easy to fix
I'm not easy to understand

I'm not easy to be around with

There's no remedy
There's no time

There's only consciousness
And external stimuli

There's only reality

I live because I breathe
I exist because I think

Bare minimum

As long as I have you in my head I am a prisoner of these
ideas
That don't rest
They don't flow
Meaningless
But powerful
Although leaving me powerless
You see they don't flow
They don't make sense

I lost my mind.

But I slowly find myself within these lines

In words that torment like a hex
Words that make me contort as if I'm possessed

I find myself in a frenzy
Delirious
Confined.

But I slowly find myself within these lines
Words that also heal as if they were divine
My ark
My salvation
The realization that I will come out of this alive.
I survived.
I will endure this pain alone
Without you or anyone
I will be transformed.
It's all thanks to you that I will be reborn
Thank you
brahmin of a selfish caste
Pretentious prince of the south
Prince of my fucking past

Although it kills me in the inside to know you will never read
these lines
You will never know the effect you had over me.
Maybe at the same time it brings me solace...
To know that at least you will not devalue my thoughts...
At least I know you they are safeguarded by the pages of this
book.
A book you will probably never touch
And if you do
At least I can rest knowing you'll have no chance to burn this
work of art, because words have power, and that power now
lies within the hands of others

Words have power
Once spoken they vanish
But engraved in a thousand other pages they will remain
lavished

I can finally say I won at least *this battle.*

You will never know…
What you caused me in the inside…

To write like Nietzsche with syphilis
And Kirk Cobain on crack
Yes.
Indeed.
The sick rabid mind of a woman who was in love…
Not even Edgar Allen Poe's raven could complete with that.
This violently happy woman who was in love
Wrote and wrote and wrote
Like lyrics to a Bjørk song menacingly inspired…
Connected to an IV of Moroccan hashish…

Flowing sublimely yet cathartically wild….

Inspirational aneurysm.

Aspirational regret.

End.

14. Fuck It Poetically

This type of love
Stays in books
Flows in music
But is then regurgitated by you
Fuck you
And the birds that chirp every morning
Fuck them too
What good morning?
Someone like you just treated me like shit
And I still sing for you
Stupid birds
Stupid violets
Stupidity doesn't begin to describe our notion of love.
Fuck love
And fuck humanity
But friendship ?
Yeah fuck that too
Ship that friend back to Timbuktu
He wanted me to go away
And I just wanted to know why
Why me?
Why did I deserve so much hatred?
So much that he couldn't say goodbye
I was worthy of an intro
Even for one night
But I wasn't worthy of a seamless gentle exit
Fuck me
Fuck my life
Fuck everyone
Fuck my world
Fuck your world
Fuck the fact that no matter what you do I will still love you

Fuck the fact that no matter what you do I will still write inspired about you
You were my world
But the pain radiating from the core of my chest was fucking childish to you
Fuck you
You want me to grow the fuck up
I want you to grow a fucking heart
Fuck my fucked up mind for still thinking about you
Fuck my fucked up mind for desiring you
Fuck my fucked up mind for understanding you.
Fuck this misery.
Fuck my poetry
Fuck my songs
Fuck my voice
Everything is fucking meaningless
When not only do you have unrequited love
You have also unrequited respect
Unrequited attention
Unrequited kindness
And unrequited humanity.

Fuck me. Fuck my life. Fuck my mind. Fuck my insanity.

Go ahead.
Feel sorry for me.
Go ahead laugh

One day the world you thought you knew will fucking laugh right back at you. End.

15. Incomprehensible

No one will ever understand what he meant for me
His smile was contagious
It still flashes before my eyes
I still caress his image with my mind

He had spunk
A special kind of devilish energy
But a pseudo innocent aura

Indispensable
Unforgettable
Irreplaceable
But Shameless
Ruthless
I couldn't get him to change
Shameless
Ruthless
He couldn't understand
Shameless
Ruthless
His kindness was an infectious lie.

16. Sacred Amulet

"I will carry him in my heart wherever he goes he will be with me like a coin like an amulet"

These lines of a beautiful Italian song were in my head for months.

"These friends keep talking way to much , say I should give him up…"

Yeah even those kinds of songs you will never find yourself actually singing to, I sang.

I sang romantic ones, and the stupid shallow ones with so much passion.

I sang. And for him I danced. I would wake up every morning excited to feel this way. Excited to feel love.

I knew it was a risk. To tell the universe I loved you.

I knew it was even a greater risk, to tell you.

But it was a risk I was willing to take.

Oh how I wish I could hear that deep compelling voice again.
I would give anything to be in your arms again
Oh how I wish I could see those dark eyes again
I would give anything to touch that warm golden skin again
Oh how I wish I could hear him calling me beautiful again
I would give anything

ANYTHING

For him to love me just a little...
For him to miss me just a little...
For him to desire me just a little...
For him to prove me wrong...

To prove to me that he is actually a good kind person
To explain to me that there are things I do not know nor
understand...

Anything to make me stop hating him.

Anything to make this pain go away.

I still love him

The secret is out

He is my sacred amulet that I wear over my scars

End.

17. Fragmented Memories, Fragmented Nostalgia

You were someone I remembered vividly yet faintly from a not so far past.

If feels terrible to remember someone this much

To then realize the falsehood of that reality

A fragmented reality.

I feel so demented.

I feel so vulnerable.

I feel so defeated.

I feel so broken.

What do I do with these shards of flashbacks?

What do I do with these fragments of happiness ?

They simply do not belong in the equation.

They don't make any sense anymore.

Your smile lingers in my mind.

I close my eyes and you are still there

I open my eyes and you are still here.

A beautiful sensation

A beautiful souvenir

Murdered

Shattered

Annihilated

Completely gone…

How will I deal with this fragmented nostalgia?

It has no *logia*…

The *nostos* is lost

And the Algos?

Well.. the *algos* in *algia* is definitely augmented

Heightened

Beyond hope

Beyond repair.

Tight spaces

Little squares

Like pixels of a Windows 98 computer

Nothing is clear.

A dreamlike sensation

But inside a nightmare.

Out of body experience

Euphoric

Epic

Majestic and serene.

Turned into chaos

Bitter toxicity

I am finding out that human nature is truly vile

Catastrophic

You can reminisce over a mother or a father

A daughter or a son

But over unrequited love and unrequited kindness

Never do this

Never again!

Its simply masochistic

With overwhelmingly nauseating uneasy feelings originating from the depths on your stomach

Combined with overwhelmingly nauseating romantic thoughts originating from the depths of your soul...

It makes no sense

It has no meaning

When you can't even remember how it started

You don't even know if the person was real

You don't know what were you experiencing.

When everything felt and feels so surreal.

Unreal.

Revealed.

Unveiled.

Released.

Unleashed?

Memories racing faster than the speed of light

Thoughts falling from skyscrapers

In never-ending flight

Cursed deja-vu

But a sacred lesson learned

So be it a blessing in disguise.

Fragments of regret yet also

Fragments of delight.

End.

18. Glitch

This anger inside of me

Brings out the sharpest end of the sword

and a killer meaning to the word.

My ultimate inspiration.

My sad reality.

A melody that takes me back to that night

I was just a glitch in your matrix

But you were the perfect algorithm in mine.

I was a mere Lolita chess piece in your sapiosexual quest...

Nothing more and everything less…

I could attempt to make you a glitch in my system

A glitch in my head

A musical note that's a little off key

A window Not Responding

CLT ALT DELETE

The program closes

The music is fading

But the beat of nostalgia keeps playing

I was just a glitch in your matrix

I was not supposed to meet you?

I was not supposed to fall in love with you?

Yet here I am

And there you are..

Oblivious to the fact that I have even been forgotten

Even my worst enemy remembers me once in a while

This is the most terrible story to tell

The most painful song to sing

How deceitful my world has been

How deceitful yours must be

You have her in your life

and yet you would rather have other glitches by your side

I cried for days

I cried for weeks

I cried for months

I cried for almost one year

You have taken control of my mind for 313 days...

Yet I only had your undivided attention for two hours.

I never wanted you to love me back

I wanted you to give me my peace of mind

I do not understand you

I do not comprehend your world

I may be bizarre,

But the golden olympic medal 2024

With no deductions…

Goes to you oh protagonist of my story

With the most complicated code of them all…

End.

19. Silver Lining

The only silver lining to unrequited love, unreciprocated kindness… it makes you sing more passionately, it forces you to write compose express ideas so vividly. So perfectly.

It renders one more precise. More creative. More enticing

More of You, Less of me

The mind is fixated on you

The one who couldn't be
The mind is fixated on you
The one who couldn't say
The mind is fixated on you
The one who couldn't be kind
The mind is fixated on you
The one who couldn't reply
The mind is fixated on you
The one who couldn't love…
My mind is punishing me..
I who couldn't rewind… End.

20. Meaningless Valuable Thoughts

Imagine possessing Valuable and Meaningless thoughts at
the same time
Alive and decayed
On point but delayed
Defined as they fade…
Perception of reality betrayed

"Meaningless valuable thoughts sleep furiously at night"

Chomsky will be proud to know that now this kind of
sentence structure actually makes sense .

Grammatically correct
 idiomatically correct

Because we finally have a scenario where valuable thoughts
do not sleep peacefully at night rendering them meaningless.
They sleep furiously because there is no closure. There was
no happy ending.
And many unanswered questions
End.

21. Meaningless Love in Humanity

"I Love you in Humanity"

Again I shall repeat…

A love so innocent and pure

It is truly basic and effortless

A love so simple and kind

It is truly benign

A love so deep and sublime

It compels you to make up rhymes…

Because it is the most powerful form a love that a human could ever experience.

It is unconditional

It is forgiving

It is more meaningful than First Corinthians Thirteen

It radiates from the spleen

It crawls through the liver

It reaches the heart

And pierces the spleen…

Now you are paralyzed.

It is a Love that is also very dangerous and toxic

Unforgiving, resentful

Oxymoronic?

Moronic?

Ironic?

Illogical Passion.

From the core of our existence

From the core of our essence

We humans need to just love.

That love wants us to be kind

It wants us to heal

That love wants us to be merciful

It wants us to feel

To be human is to have empathy

To be human YOU may say..

Is to make mistakes…

To be a *wise, mature and moral* human however…

Is to admit those mistakes and ask for forgiveness.

Remorse.

Guilt.

Accountability.

This is to be human.

Still loving you despite all of this…

Is my own love for you in humanity.

These lines, these emotions are a product of you.

It is the worst and best feeling in the world.

It is a prison, yet liberating

It is exhilarating yet excruciating

It is what it is…

Flattering? Disturbing?

Don't worry… it is all meaningless at the end…

We live. We Rejoice. We Suffer. We Die.

These are just pages in a book

You will one day take for granted.

You are indefinitely undefined

Unequivocally refined

The best mystery

Yet an awful enigma

The last of this vicious cycle.

But the first of my series of epileptic literary episodes

The one that ultimately disappointed me the most.

He may never find the contents of this book.

He may have already forgotten my existence…

See how meaningless it is to love someone in humanity?

It is a love that has zero expectations.

A love that requires no relationship

No marriage

No family

No descendants..

Not childish nor shallow

Despite the bad that you make think lurks inside of you

I had faith in you.

I believed in you

I trusted you.

Prince of my Past,

I was meaningless to you

Yet you meant the world to me

Loving someone in humanity means just that..

One sided passion, uneven compassion

You love them for the sake of who they are

Not for what they can offer you

Whether you are deserving of it or not..

It does not matter.

This type of love is indiscriminate.

I loved you in humanity.

But I am now drained from all the humanity inside of me.

End.

22. Sacrificial Lamb

He drowned me in impurity

He search, he found, and he devoured

What a menace to this world.

He drowned me in darkness

He drowned me in hatred

He drowned me in so much sorrow

Down below I go

I cannot breathe

Up the surface I arise

I smile

Down below I go

Once again I am drowning

Up the surface I arise

I find a reason to be happy

But down below I go I am now trapped

Up the surface I arise I cannot escape

In and out he went

Only so that I can then sink and float.

A dead body with a faint soul

He used as a vessel for his pleasure

What was actually inside, he sacrificed.

As a Sacrificial Lamb I was used

For what she couldn't offer him.

As a Sacrificial Lamb I was used.

For what she needed to keep him closer.

Whether I live or whether I die

They did not care

Down below I go

I want to close my eyes forever

But up the surface I arise from a Mikva of clarity

I am here. I am alive. I am Purified. Revived.

A born again lamb with stains of Saffron red washed away.

End

"Women are scorpions whose sting is sweet"
-Imam Ali Abu Talib

"This is where Ziva shot her own brother, there where you are
standing…
That is closure.
The rest is just memories
Let them be memories."

-Quote from the show "NCIS" on CBS.

In Memory of Mazryah Taziri

In dedication to all of those who feel emotions intensely, to all of
those who have been wronged and never got a true sense of justice,
to all of those who suffered from a very fucked up version of
unrequited love.

Hello…? Can anyone hear me? It is very cold in this labyrinth…
Where does this hallway or door lead to?
Is that… the exit?

www.ingramcontent.com/pod-product-compliance
Lightning Source LLC
Chambersburg PA
CBHW061723020426
42331CB00006B/1070